D1347496

Coordination and text · *Coordination et rédaction* · Koordination und Redaktion
MARTHA TORRES ARCILA

Editorial Director · *Directeur éditorial* · Verlagsdirektor
Nacho Asensio

Design and layout · *Conception et maquette* · Design und Layout
Carlos Gamboa Permanyer

Cover design · *Création de page de garde* · Außengestaltung
Núria Sordé Orpinell

Translation · *Traduction* · Übersetzung
Serena Chiang (English)
Anne Ouvrard (Français)
Katrin Nell (Deutsch)

Production · *Production* · Produktion
Juanjo Rodríguez Novel

Contemporary Houses of the World

Maisons Contemporaines du Monde

MODERNE HÄUSER AUS ALLER WELT

CONTEMPORARY HOUSES OF THE WORLD
·
MAISONS CONTEMPORAINES DU MONDE
·
MODERNE HÄUSER AUS ALLER WELT

||||

Contents · Index · Inhaltsverzeichnis

Contemporary Houses of the World

The design of the single family dwelling, as a primary element of comfort and well-being, has always constituted one of the most important branches in the field of architecture. Understanding the needs of human beings as the nucleus of society and creating spaces for them of the highest architectural quality is, perhaps, one of the most ambitious man's relationships with society have also undergone transformations. It is for this reason that the design of the modern-day home implies a certain degree of difficulty while at the same time providing constant challenges: to design a home today requires an understanding of the complexities and contradictions present in the very base of society and its relationships.

challenges existing in this discipline. From residences designed to fit within a minimum amount of space to the most avant-guard proposals, man has always striven to create spaces which would protect his privacy under optimum conditions. Nonetheless, with the passage of time and as a result of society's development, important changes have occurred in the lifestyles of the world's inhabitants. Understanding these transformations also implies comprehending the changes which have occurred in the demands of the individual. Consequently,

The process of designing a home demands a high level of commitment from the architect as it implies investigating into the intimacies of the members of a family: how they eat, how they sleep, how they spend their free time... Evaluating each of these aspects and placing them within the context of the peculiarities of each commission is one of the most compelling situations which an architect must face. Various models exist within this particular branch of architecture: the isolated single-family dwelling –located on plots containing wide extensions of privately-owned green spaces, urban developments– with narrow courtyards, vacation homes –endowed with attractive views over their surroundings. In fact, the variety of conditions found in each of the projects– both in terms of their location as well as the clientele – makes it difficult to establish clear connections between them. Nonetheless, if we are to un-

tensive plots. The obvious differences between these examples make it necessary to comprehend the specific characteristics of each project in depth, which brings us closer to the personal vision of the architect.

In this manner, through an array of over 60 homes distributed throughout the world, a variety of situations reflecting the same

derstand the idea of the home as a "private space", each of the examples presented serves as an element of reference for the analysis of the individual, regardless of the diversity in the formal and spatial results achieved in the different residences.

This book proposes a review of numerous projects constructed in recent years within the branch of single family dwellings, from houses built between party walls as part of great residential complexes, to isolated single family projects located on ex-

theme is presented from different points of view: situations involving cultural differences (including projects from various continents), architectural developments (the existence of different formal solutions to similar conditions) and changes in lifestyle (with unusual program proposals). All these factors lead us to verify the transformations and complexities of the human being within the most personal inhabitable space which one can own: a home.

MARTHA TORRES ARCILA

INTRODUCTION

MAISONS CONTEMPORAINES DU MONDE

L e concept de maison individuelle, principal élément de confort et de bien-être pour l'homme, a toujours constitué l'une des recherches les plus importantes en architecture. Parvenir à comprendre les besoins de chacun au sein de notre société et créer des espaces de la plus haute qualité architecturale est peut-être l'un des défis les plus ambitieux dans

conception d'une habitation implique difficultés et défis : être capable d'apprécier les complexités et les contradictions de la base même de la société et leur relations.

Le processus d'élaboration d'une maison requiert un grand engagement de la part de l'architecte, car il s'agit de faire des recherches sur l'intimité des membres d'une fa-

cette discipline. Des maisons conçues à partir de peu de moyens jusqu'aux propositions avant-gardistes, on a toujours cherché à créer des espaces permettant de préserver l'intimité dans les meilleures conditions. Cependant, au fil des ans, et avec le développement des sociétés, d'importants changements sont intervenus dans le mode de vie humain. Comprendre ces changements signifie comprendre les changements qui se produisent dans les exigences de chacun. Dès lors, leurs rapports avec la société sont altérés, et la

mille : comprendre comment ils mangent, comment ils dorment, comment ils profitent de leur temps libre... Evaluer tous ces aspects et les mettre en contexte à l'intérieur des caractéristiques de chaque commande est l'une des situations les plus intéressantes auxquelles doit faire face l'architecte. On compte différents modèles dans cette typologie, de la maison individuelle isolée – où la disposition des terrains permet de grands espaces verts privés – aux développements urbains où l'on trouve d'étroits patios, en passant par les résidences secondaires avec de très belles vues sur le paysage environnant. Chaque projet présentant des conditions particulières, aussi bien par rapport au lieu que du point de vue du client, il est difficile d'établir des connexions précises entres eux. Néanmoins, si l'on appréhende le concept de maison en tant qu'''espace d'intimité'', tous les exemples servent d'élément de référence à l'analyse

ractéristiques spécifiques à chaque projet, ce qui permet de nous rapprocher de la vision de l'architecte lui-même.

Ainsi, et à travers plus de soixante projets répartis dans le monde entier, nous tâcherons de présenter, selon divers points de vue, la multiplicité des situations reflétées dans une même thématique : les différen-

de l'individu, indépendamment des résultats variés quant aux formes et aux espaces de l'habitation.

Ce livre aborde de nombreux projets construits au cours des dernières années dans la typologie du logement individuel, qui s'étendent de la maison mitoyenne à l'intérieur d'importants complexes résidentiels jusqu'aux projets individuels isolés sur de grands terrains. Les différences manifestes entre toutes les maisons proposées dans cet ouvrage nous font comprendre les ca-

ces culturelles (des projets élaborés dans plusieurs continents), les changements propres à l'architecture (les différentes solutions formelles adoptées dans des conditions semblables), et les modifications dans les habitudes de vie (propositions programmatiques insolites). Tous ces facteurs nous aideront à discerner les transformations et les complexités de l'homme au sein de l'espace habitable le plus personnel qu'il ait en sa possession : la maison.

MARTHA TORRES ARCILA

INTRODUCTION

MODERNE HÄUSER AUS ALLER WELT

D as Design des Einfamilienhauses –ein grundlegender Bestandteil von Komfort und Wohlbehagen des Menschen– war schon immer eine der wichtigsten Forschungsgebiete in der Architektur. So ist es möglicherweise eine der interessantesten Herausforderungen dieser Branche, die Bedürfnisse des Menschen als Kern der Gesellschaft zu verstehen und für ihn Räume höchster ar-

eingehen. Da sich also auch seine gesellschaftlichen Beziehungen ändern, ist das Design eines Wohnhauses ein kritisches Thema und eine Herausforderung, denn man sollte die Komplexität, die Widersprüche und die Beziehungen in der Gesellschaft verstehen.

Der Prozess des Entwurfes eines Wohnhauses erfordert vom Architekten sehr viel Feinfüh-

chitektonischer Qualität zu schaffen. Angefangen bei Wohnhäusern, deren Design auf Mindestmaßen basiert, bis hin zu den avantgardistischen Planungen ist es immer erstrebenswert, Räume zu schaffen, in denen die Möglichkeit geboten wird, die Privatsphäre unter optimalen Bedingungen zu entwickeln. Im Verlaufe der Jahre und mit dem Wandel der Gesellschaft haben sich auch im Lebenswandel der Menschen entscheidende Änderungen vollzogen. Wenn man diese Änderungen versteht, dann kann man auch auf die sich veränderten Bedürfnisse des Menschen

ligkeit, denn er muss darüber hinaus über die Privatsphäre einer Familie informiert sein, zum Beispiel über ihre Ess- und Schlafgewohnheiten oder über ihre Freizeitaktivitäten. Die Wertschätzung all dieser Aspekte und ihre Einordnung in die Besonderheiten jedes Auftrages ist eine der interessantesten Situationen, der ein Architekt in dieser Typologie gegenübersteht. Die Typologie schließt mehrere Modelle ein: einzeln stehende Einfamilienhäuser mit Grundstücken, auf denen weiträumige private Grünflächen angelegt werden können, Erschließungen von Wohnsiedlungen mit engen Innenhöfen oder auch Ferienhäuser mit herrlichen Aussichten über die Gegend, in der sie sich befinden. Durch die unterschiedlichen Bedingungen, die bei jedem einzelnen Projekt sowohl durch den Standort als auch durch den Auftraggeber bestimmt werden, ist es natürlich schwierig, zwischen den Projekten klare Verbindungen zu erstellen. Wenn jedoch jedes Haus als privater Bereich betrach-

die klaren Unterschiede zwischen den verschiedenen Häusern ist es notwendig, die individuellen Eigenschaften jedes Projektes zu verstehen, wodurch die eigene Sichtweise des Architekten deutlich wird.

In mehr als 60 Projekten aus allen Teilen der Welt wird aus verschiedenen Sichtweisen die Vielschichtigkeit der Situationen dargestellt,

tet wird, dient jedes einzelne der hier angeführten Beispiele als Referenz zur Analyse des einzelnen Menschen, unabhängig davon, dass formelle und räumliche Gestaltung der Wohnhäuser voneinander abweichen.

Dieses Buch enthält eine Übersicht über eine Vielzahl in den letzten Jahren entwickelter Projekte im Bereich der Einfamilienhäuser, angefangen bei Reihenhäusern, die zu großen Wohnungsbauerschließungen gehören bis hin zu einzeln stehenden Einfamilienhäusern mit weiträumigen Grundstücken. Durch

die sich in einer gemeinsamen Thematik wiederfinden. Die kulturellen Unterschiede (die Projekte befinden sich auf unterschiedlichen Kontinenten), eigene Varianten in der Architektur (mit unterschiedlichen formellen Anordnungen unter ähnlichen Bedingungen) und Abwandlungen in der Lebensweise (unübliche Programmplanungen). Durch all diese Faktoren werden sowohl Änderungen als auch die Komplexität des Menschen in seinem intim-sten bewohnbaren Raum deutlich: das Haus.

MARTHA TORRES ARCILA

EINLEITUNG

CASA A-M

ELENA MATEU POMAR, ARQUITECTO

Barcelona, España. 1998 / 1999-2001

The steep incline of the plot with attractive views over the city of Barcelona is one of the main conditioning factors in this project. In order to fully exploit this situation, a composition of successive volumes and walls, which adapt themselves to the terrain by using its unevenness to their advantage, is proposed. This dissipation of the elements according to the topography permits an optimum organization of the functional program. However, in the course of developing the project, each and every one of the rooms in the building is successfully reunified in order to create a unitary element upon the mountainside.

La forte pente de ce terrain, avec de très belles vues sur Barcelone, est l'une des conditions déterminantes de ce projet. Afin d'exploiter cette situation, l'auteur propose une composition de volumes et de plans qui se suivent en s'adaptant au terrain de manière à tirer le meilleur parti des dénivellations. Les éléments se dissolvent suivant la topographie, ce qui permet une organisation optimale du programme fonctionnel. Toutes ces pièces sont toutefois rassemblées pendant l'élaboration du projet pour faire de celui-ci un ensemble unitaire sur la montagne.

Die starke Neigung des Grundstücks mit herrlichen Aussichten über die Stadt Barcelona ist eines der Hauptkriterien dieses Projektes. Um diese Situation zu nutzen, werden Baukörper und Grundrisse in einer Reihe angeordnet. Durch diese Anpassung an das Gelände werden dessen Unebenheiten optimal genutzt. Durch diese der Topografie entsprechenden Anordnung der Elemente wird eine perfekte Organisierung der funktionellen Planung ermöglicht. In der Entwicklungsphase des Projektes werden jedoch alle Abschnitte des Gesamtwerkes miteinander verbunden, sodass sie als ein einziges Element inmitten des Gebirges wahrgenommen werden.

CASA A-M

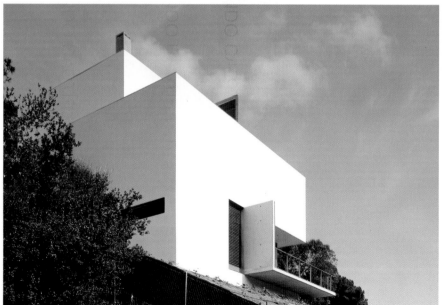

A route based on groups of stairways resolves the question of the vertical connections between the different levels of the house.

Un parcours d'escaliers assure la connexion verticale entre les différents niveaux de la maison.

Durch mehrere Treppengänge werden die vertikalen Verbindungen zwischen den verschiedenen Etagen des Hauses hergestellt.

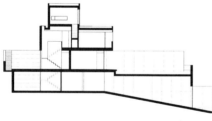

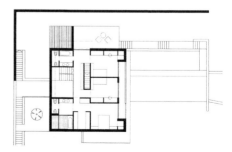

ALLGAIER HOUSE

B & E BAUMSCHLAGER-EBERLE

Lochau, Österreich. 1996 / 1996-1998

In the opinion of these architects, a project should be the result of the specific conditions involved in its conception, from the management to the budget, rather than merely an architectural fact. They see their architectural responsibility as a symbiosis between constructive logic and a formal typological study along with a control of the "external" variables. This single-family dwelling reflects the polished development of each of these aspects. It was conceived as one sole volume, although its interior has been designed for three uses: a house, an apartment and an office. Subtle façade designs and the introduction of a glazed bridge provide hints to the interior organization as seen from the outside.

Pour ces architectes, un projet doit, au-delà de l'aspect architectural, être le résultat des circonstances précises dans lesquelles il a été conçu, de la gestion jusqu'au budget. Leur œuvre architecturale est une symbiose entre la logique constructive et l'étude typologique et formelle, de pair avec un contrôle des variables "extérieures". Cette demeure individuelle reflète l'élaboration raffinée de chacun de ces aspects. La conception du volume est unique, et son intérieur est organisé de manière à réunir trois fonctions : celles de maison, d'appartement et de bureau. Le subtil travail sur la façade et l'incorporation d'un pont vitré suggèrent l'organisation intérieure depuis la rue.

Diese Architekten betrachten ein Projekt wohl nicht nur aus architektonischer Sicht, sondern darüber hinaus auch die spezifischen Bedingungen, unter denen es entwickelt wurde, von den Formalitäten bis hin zum Kostenvoranschlag. Ihr architektonisches Wirken ist eine Symbiose zwischen konstruktiver Logik und der Studie von Typologie und Formen, begleitet von der Kontrolle der "externen" Variablen. In diesem Einfamilienhaus spiegelt sich bis ins kleinste Detail die Entwicklung jedes einzelnen dieser Aspekte wider. Sein Baukörper wird als Einheit wahrgenommen, obgleich die Innenraumnutzung in ein Haus, eine Wohnung und ein Büro eingeteilt ist. Eine raffinierte Gestaltung der Fassaden und eine verglaste Brücke deuten dem äußeren Betrachter die Anordnung des Inneren an.

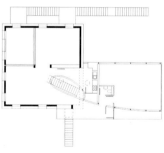

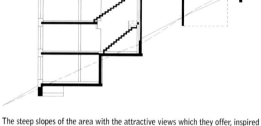

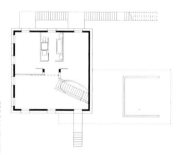

The steep slopes of the area with the attractive views which they offer, inspired the construction of the houses at the upper end of the plots. Thus, it is not unusual to discover houses typologically based on towers, emerging out of the slope.

Les grandes inclinaisons de ce quartier aux vues attrayantes suggèrent la construction de logements sur la partie élevée du terrain. Il n'est donc pas étonnant de voir des maisons qui utilisent comme base la typologie des tours, qui émergent de la pente.

Wegen der steilen Neigungen des Gebietes mit seinen herrlichen Ausblicken wurden die Häuser auf dem oberen Abschnitt der Grundstücke gebaut. Somit ist es nicht untypisch, dass Häuser entstehen, deren Typologie auf Türmen basiert, die auf dem Abhang emporragen.

ANOTHER GLASS HOUSE BETWEEN SEA AND SKY

SHOEI YOH + ARCHITECTS

Fukuoka, Japan. 1991

In this house situated atop a cliff 140 m. above the sea, the design in cantilever permits the construction of an almost sculptural volume, which "levitates" over the mountain. The imposing presence of two walls which serve as anchorage contrasts formally with the transparency and lightness of the volume which defies gravity as it projects itself directly towards the cliff. During development of the project, the search for transparency in the structure led to its decomposition: rather than merely a crystalline "box", it is a structure which dissolves into two horizontal elements, the roof and the floor, which are separated by imperceptible glazed walls.

La structure en porte-à-faux de cette maison, située sur une falaise 140m au-dessus de la mer, permet l'élaboration d'un volume quasiment sculptural, "en lévitation" sur la montagne. La présence imposante de deux murs, qui servent d'ancrage, est compensée par la transparence et la légèreté du bâtiment, qui défie la pesanteur en se projetant juste au-dessus de la falaise. Pendant la réalisation du projet, la recherche des transparences a permis de le décomposer : plus qu'un volume cristallin, cette œuvre se fond en deux éléments horizontaux – le toit et le sol – séparés par d'imperceptibles vitrages.

Dieses Haus wurde an einer Steilküste in einer Höhe von 140 m über dem Meer gebaut. Durch die Auskragungen wird die Errichtung eines nahezu strukturellen Baukörpers ermöglicht, der förmlich über dem Hügel schwebt. Der Beständigkeit zweier Mauern, die als Verankerung dienen, wirken die Transparenz und Leichtigkeit des Baukörpers entgegen, wodurch die Schwerkraft herausgefordert wird, da er sich direkt an der Steilküste befindet. In der Entwicklungsphase des Projekts führte die Suche nach Transparenz im Baukörper schließlich zu seiner Aufteilung. Der gläserne "Block" ist horizontal in zwei Elemente, Decke und Fußboden, aufgeteilt, die durch kaum wahrnehmbare verglaste Flächen voneinander getrennt werden.

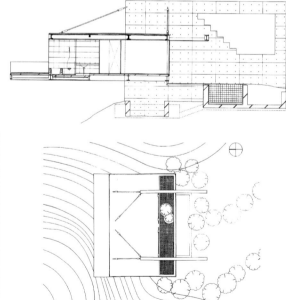

Apart from the complex relations established with the cliff, the design of the floor plan in the residence is of great simplicity, allowing for a flexible use of the space which opens out completely towards breath-taking views over the sea.

Au-delà des relations complexes établies avec la falaise, le schéma structurel de la demeure reste d'une grande simplicité, permettant un usage flexible de l'espace, qui s'ouvre complètement aux vues privilégiées sur la mer.

Trotz der verflochtenen Bezüge zur Steilküste ist das Design der Innenräume des Wohnhauses sehr einfach gehalten. Dies ermöglicht eine flexible Nutzung des Raumes, der sich vollkommen den einzigartigen Ausblicken auf das Meer öffnet.

VILLA A BERNAREGGIO

MARIO BOTTA ARCHITETTO

Milano, Italia. 1991-1996 / 1995-2000

Due to the physical conditions in the area, this project was destined *a-priori* to become a landmark on the plain where it is located. Hence, this intervention comprising 10 houses and a villa was proposed to mark the boundaries of the city, creating a wall within the urban confines. Nonetheless the villa, isolated as a crowning element, enjoys greater freedom in its formal and spatial treatment. Separated from the remainder of the colony by a small, private road, it boasts a clearly ordered form with simple and forceful lines.

Par rapport aux conditions géographiques du lieu, ce projet devait a priori former une délimitation à l'intérieur d'une plaine. Cette composition de dix maisons et d'une villa s'instaure telle la limite de la ville, formant une muraille à ses confins. Cependant, la villa isolée, en tant qu'élément final, jouit d'une plus grande liberté dans son traitement des formes et de l'espace. Séparée du complexe par une petite rue à usage privée, elle se compose d'une géométrie parfaitement ordonnée de lignes simples et tranchantes.

Aufgrund der physischen Beschaffenheit der ebenen Landschaft, von der das Projekt umgeben ist, sollte es an diesem Standort *a priori* zu einem Meilenstein werden. So wurde die Errichtung von zehn Häusern und einer Villa so geplant, als handele es sich um die Begrenzung einer Stadt, einer Stadtmauer ähnlich. Nur beim Entwurf der abgelegenen Villa, das abschließende Element, hat man sich mehr Freiheit in der formellen und räumlichen Gestaltung eingeräumt. Sie wird durch eine kleine Privatstrasse von den anderen Häusern getrennt und wurde mittels einer klar definierten Geometrie mit einfachen und überzeugenden Linien errichtet.

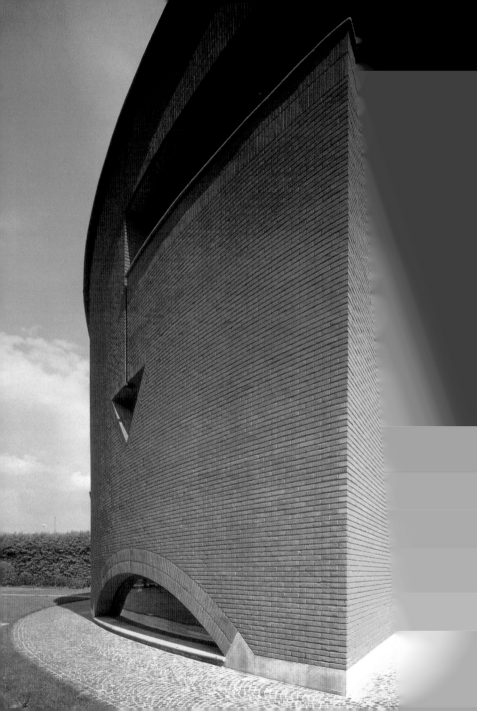

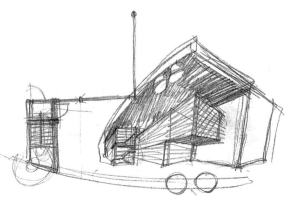

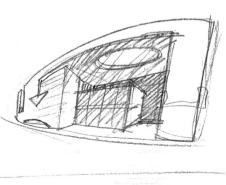

The architectural commitment to the surroundings is clearly perceptible in this proposal upon observing the placement of this residence which, apart from the solutions presented on an individual level, has become an important element defining the edge of the city.

On perçoit dans ce projet le compromis architectural en respect du lieu à travers l'implantation d'un ensemble qui, au-delà de sa solution spécifique, représente un important élément limitrophe avec la ville.

In dieser Planung wird der Kompromiss zwischen Architektur und Standort durch die Eingliederung des Gesamtwerkes wahrgenommen, das nicht nur einen stilvollen Eindruck macht, sondern durch das außerdem die Stadt begrenzt wird.

VILLA A BERNAREGGIO

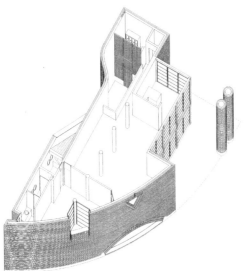

The work of this Swiss architect has always been characterized by a profound respect for the locations where he intervenes. His architectural language has enjoyed the influence of two great masters of world architecture: Louis Kahn and Carlo Scarpa.

L'œuvre de cet architecte suisse se caractérise par un respect constant du lieu où doit s'ériger la construction. Son langage architectural s'inspire de deux grands maîtres de l'architecture mondiale : Louis Kahn et Carlo Scarpa.

Das Werk dieses schweizerischen Architekten zeichnete sich immer durch einen tiefen Respekt zu dem Standort aus, in den es eingreift. Seine architektonische Sprache wurde durch zwei große Meister der weltweiten Architektur, Louis Kahn und Carlo Scarpa, beeinflusst.

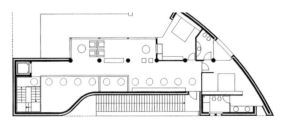

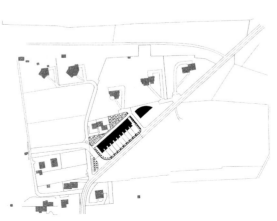

HOUSE IN BESAZIO

GIOVANNI GUSCETTI

Besazio, Switzerland. 2001

This residence is located in the region of Mendrisiotto, a residential district characterized by great stretches of terrain with generous green spaces. Preserving the maximum amount of vegetation was one of the bases for the proposal of this dwelling. Thanks to a detailed study of the natural conditions existing on the plot, it was possible to build the house while scarcely altering the characteristics of this plot. This factor also contributed to the determination of the planimetry: one of the corners of the house was removed in order to create a courtyard which would allow for the conservation of an existing tree. The functional program was organized within a single volume with large expanses of glass which facilitate a profound relationship with the exterior.

Cette habitation se situe dans la région de Mendrisiotto, zone résidentielle caractérisée par de grandes terrasses entourées d'espaces verts. Préserver la végétation a été l'une des conditions de base pour l'élaboration de cette maison. Après une étude détaillée des conditions naturelles du terrain, la maison a pu être construite pratiquement sans altérer ces caractéristiques, ce qui a également conditionné la planimétrie : un des angles se vide pour créer un patio qui permet de maintenir un arbre en vie. Le programme fonctionnel s'organise au sein d'un volume unique, avec de grandes surfaces vitrées qui créent un lien solide avec l'extérieur.

Dieses Wohnhaus befindet sich in der Region von Mendrisiotto, ein Wohngebiet, das sich durch große Grundstücke mit weiträumigen Grünflächen auszeichnet. Für die Planung des Wohnhauses wurde der Maßstab gesetzt, diese Vegetation möglichst zu erhalten. Als Ergebnis der genauen Studien über die natürlichen Bedingungen des Grundstücks wurde das Haus fast ohne Beeinträchtigung dieser Beschaffenheit errichtet. Dadurch wurde auch die Planimetrie beeinflusst, denn es wurde auf einen der Eckpunkte des Hauses verzichtet und stattdessen ein Innenhof geschaffen, auf dem Platz für einen Baum geboten wird. Die funktionelle Anordnung beruht auf einem einzigen Baukörper mit großen verglasten Flächen, durch die eine enge Beziehung zur äußeren Umgebung entsteht.

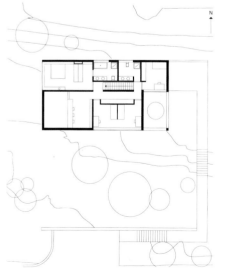

The design of the windows as large glazed walls accentuates the absence of barriers between the interior and exterior.

Les fenêtres, qui prennent la forme de grandes surfaces vitrées, font ressortir l'absence de barrières avec l'extérieur.

Durch die Gestaltung der Fenster als große Glasflächen wird betont, dass es keine Grenzen zur äußeren Umgebung gibt.

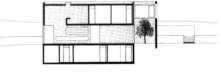

The materials used emphasize the simplicity of the project. Plaster, ceramics and wood are used in the interior.

Les matériaux utilisés mettent en valeur la simplicité du projet. L'intérieur est composé de plâtre, céramique et bois.

Durch den Einsatz der Materialien wird die Einfachheit des Projektes betont. Im Innenraum wird Gips, Keramik und Holz verwendet.

The house is organized within a single volume whose relationship with the exterior was the decisive factor in its formal treatment: large expanses of glass replace the windows.

La maison s'organise en un volume unique, dont la relation avec l'extérieur influence directement le traitement des formes : de grandes ouvertures vitrées remplacent les fenêtres.

Das Haus besteht aus einem einzigen Baukörper, dessen Beziehung zur äußeren Umgebung durch die formelle Anordnung bestimmt wird, die durch große verglaste Öffnungen als Ersatz für die Fenster besticht.

BÖHLER-JUTZ HOUSE

B & E BAUMSCHLAGER-EBERLE

Dorbirn, Österreich. 1996 / 1996-1998

A large part of the professional practice of Baumschlager & Eberle has dealt with the sector of single-family dwellings. One of the keys to their accurate solutions lies in their quest for perfecting these dwellings rather than in the need for innovation in each project. This allows them to take each new project "one step further". As in other cases, for this dwelling a single volume which would present the initial impression of the residence as a whole was proposed. Nonetheless, a second elongated volume was subsequently anchored to the main structure. Thus a line was created parallel to the edge of the hillside, which made it possible to enjoy the views from the location.

Une grande partie de la pratique professionnelle de Baumschlager & Eberle s'est développée en suivant la typologie des habitations unifamiliales. Une des clés pour parvenir à ce résultat réside davantage dans la quête du perfectionnement de ces œuvres que dans le besoin d'innover pour chacune d'entre elles. Ceci leur permet d'aller plus loin pour chaque nouveau projet. Ce logement, de même que d'autres réalisés auparavant, comprend un volume unique, qui donne l'image initiale de l'ensemble. Toutefois, un deuxième élément aux proportions élargies vient s'ancrer au volume principal, ce qui crée une ligne parallèle à la limite de la pente et permet ainsi de tirer parti du paysage d'un point de vue spatial.

Baumschlager & Eberle gewannen den Großteil ihrer beruflichen Praxis innerhalb der Typologie der Einfamilienhäuser. Der Schlüssel für ihre treffenden Lösungen ist der Suche nach Perfektion derselben, nicht so sehr in der Notwendigkeit der Innovation jeder einzelnen. Dadurch ist es ihnen möglich, mit jedem neuen Projekt "einen Schritt voraus zu gehen". Wie auch bei anderen Projekten sieht die Planung für dieses Wohnhaus einen einzigen Baukörper vor, der dem Gesamtwerk den ersten Eindruck verleiht. Ein zweiter Baukörper mit länglichen Proportionen wird an den zentralen Block angeschlossen. Damit wird eine Linie parallel zum Abhang geschaffen, durch die man die Ausblicke auf die Umgebung auf traumhafte Weise genießen kann.

On the floor plan, the second volume becomes an elongated element penetrating into the main structure. The asymmetric lines thus produced clearly differentiate the "noble" areas of the residence.

A l'intérieur, le deuxième volume se transforme en un élément allongé qui pénètre dans le premier étage. L'asymétrie produite permet de différencier nettement les espaces nobles de la propriété.

Der zweite Baukörper ist im Grundriss ein längliches Element, das an den zentralen Baukörper anknüpft. Durch die somit erzeugte Asymmetrie wird eine deutliche Abteilung der stilvollen Räume des Wohnhauses ermöglicht.

The formal proposal is based upon a single volume with orthogonal lines which provides order to the dwelling. A second element "crossing" the structure on one side anchors it in place.

La structure formelle est basée sur un volume unique de lignes orthogonales qui organisent le plan de la maison. Un second élément "traverse" un des côtés pour rejoindre le volume qu'il relie au reste de l'ensemble.

Die formelle Planung des Wohnhauses basiert auf einem einzigen Baukörper orthogonal angeordneter Linien. Ein zweites Element durchbricht auf einer Seite den Baukörper, der die Verankerung zum Standort ist.

House on Borneo Sporenburg-Plot 12

MVRDV, Joost Glissenaar, Bart Spee, Alex Brouwer

Amsterdam, The Netherlands. 1996 / 2000

This house forms a part of the residential development on Borneo Sporenburg to the east of Amsterdam. The possibility of parcelling out the land into elongated plots was carried out to its greatest expression here. The 5 m. width of the plot was used in part on the floor plan to form an elongated strip to which one or two areas —depending on the level— were annexed. This narrow strip was transformed into a glazed box from which two hermetic structures were "hung" at different heights, thus creating a path for private use. Above this path, in addition to the two structures, a third element was designed: a box located below street level, whose inclined roof forms an access ramp to the garage.

Cette maison fait partie du complexe résidentiel de Borneo Sporenburg à l'est d'Amsterdam. Les possibilités de lotissement sur des terrains aux proportions allongées sont ici exploitées à leur maximum. Les 5m de large du terrain sont en partie utilisés par une bande allongée à laquelle se rattachent, selon la hauteur, un ou deux espaces. Cette bande étroite forme un ensemble vitré auquel "s'accrochent" deux blocs hermétiques de hauteur différente, ce qui forme un passage à usage privé. En plus des deux volumes, un troisième élément s'organise, dont le toit incliné, audessous du niveau de la rue, devient une place de parking.

Dieses Haus ist Bestandteil der Wohnraumerschließung in Borneo Sporenburg, östlich von Amsterdam. Die Möglichkeiten der Parzellierung in Grundstücke länglicher Proportionen werden hier vollkommen ausgeschöpft. Die Grundstücksbreite von 5 m wird zum Teil genutzt, was durch einen länglichen Abschnitt ermöglicht wird, an den je nach Höhe ein oder zwei Räume angeschlossen sind. Dieser schmale Abschnitt besteht aus einem Baukörper aus Glas, von dem zwei geschlossene Baukörper auf verschiedenen Höhen "herabhängen", wodurch eine kleine private Straße entsteht. Auf dieser ist außer der zwei Baukörper noch ein drittes Element angeordnet, ein Block unter der Strasse, dessen schräges Dach eine Rampe zu den Garagen bildet.

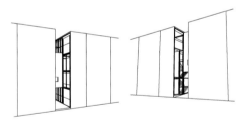

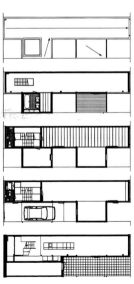

The two semi-detached volumes introduce spatial variations into the house. One of these volumes becomes the guestroom with its own bath, the other permits the expansion of two studios on the first and second levels.

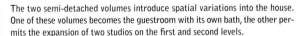

Les deux volumes qui constituent la maison offrent une grande diversité spatiale. Le premier est une chambre d'amis avec salle de bains, et l'autre permet de gagner de l'espace pour les deux studios situés au premier et deuxième étage.

Durch die beiden in Reihe angeordneten Baukörper wird die räumliche Abwechslung des Hauses ermöglicht. In einem Baukörper befindet sich das Gästezimmer mit Bad und durch den anderen wird in der ersten und zweiten Etage eine Erweiterung durch jeweils ein Büro geboten.

HOUSE ON BORNEO SPORENBURG-PLOT 18

MVRDV, JOOST GLISSENAAR, BART SPEE, ALEX BROUWER, FRANS DE WITTE

Amsterdam, The Netherlands. 1996 / 1999

The area of Borneo Sporenburg is the result of the urban planning project developed by West 8 Landscape Architects. A row of 60 dwellings, each with its own plots and specific conditions, was planned for this urban project. Within the parcelling plan, number 18 was a garden plot. For this reason 4 m. of green space on the canal side were required for the proposal in order to comply with the local regulations. The tight measurements of the plot (4,2 m. × 16 m.) and its use as a garden made it necessary to study the spatial exploitation to the utmost. Thus, an intermediate volume "slides" towards the canal within a glazed box in order to create a spacious longitudinal section.

La zone de Bornéo Sporenburg est le résultat du plan d'urbanisme développé par West 8 Landscape Architects. Une rangée de 60 logements en parcelles aux caractéristiques spécifiques est prévue pour ce projet urbain. A l'intérieur du lotissement, le numéro 18 est constitué d'un jardin, d'où la nécessité de laisser un espace vert de 4m jusqu'au canal, pour respecter la réglementation. Les mesures adaptées de la parcelle (4,2 m × 16 m) et son caractère de jardin ont engendré une étude minutieuse de l'utilisation de l'espace. A l'intérieur de la section vitrée, un volume intermédiaire "glisse" jusqu'au canal, créant ainsi une section longitudinale spacieuse.

Die Gegend von Borneo Sporenburg entstand im Rahmen des Städtebaus, der von West 8 Landscape Architects durchgeführt wurde. In diesem städtischen Projekt sind 60 in Reihe angeordnete Wohnhäuser mit Grundstücken und spezifischen Bedingungen vorgesehen. Da die Nummer 18 der Parzellierung ein Gartengrundstück war, musste die Planung gemäß der Normen eine 4 m breite Grünfläche zum Kanal hin einbeziehen. Wegen der engen Grundstücksmaße (4,2 × 16 m) und seinem Nutzen als Garten wurde die Raumnutzung besonders berücksichtigt. In einem Baukörper aus Glas ist ein zweiter mit Ausrichtung und Öffnung zum Kanal angeordnet, wodurch ein großräumiger länglicher Abschnitt entsteht.

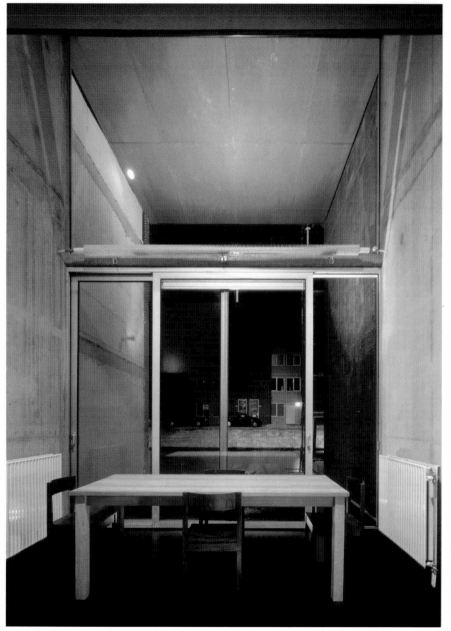

Displacing the greater part of the volume towards the back of the house permitted the possibilities of the lot to be exploited to the fullest. On the inside, this displacement creates an attractive spatial sequence.

Le volume étant déplacé jusqu'à l'arrière de la maison, on peut tirer parti des possibilités du terrain. A l'intérieur, ce mouvement crée une séquence spatiale fascinante.

Durch das Verlegen des grösseren Baukörpers auf den hinteren Teil des Hauses können die Möglichkeiten des Grundstücks maximal genutzt werden, während im Inneren eine attraktive räumliche Sequenz geschaffen wird.

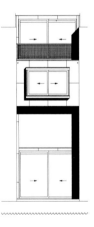

CANYON RESIDENCE

STEVEN EHRLICH ARCHITECTS

California, USA. 1999

The architecture of this designer reflects, on the one hand, the importance of the relationships between the buildings and their surroundings, and on the other hand, the diverse influences present in his work: from vernacular architecture and its particular elements to the most recent architectural styles and their formal expressions. This house establishes strong connections with its location, whose attractions —including a number of trees "typical" of the region— are "included" within the project. The L-shaped planimetry permitted the recovery of the idea of a courtyard, although in this case one of the sides was opened up in order to extend the boundaries of the house. The formal proposal is based upon a composition of lines, planes and cubes reminiscent of the Neoplasticist artwork of the first third of the twentieth century.

L'architecture de cet auteur reflète, d'un côté, l'importance des relations entre les constructions et le lieu où elles sont implantées, et de l'autre, les sources variées qui influencent son œuvre, depuis l'architecture vernaculaire et ses éléments jusqu'aux créations plus récentes et leur expression formelle. De fortes connexions s'établissent ici entre la maison et le lieu environnant, où les nombreux arbres typiques de la région qui forment le paysage sont "compris" dans le projet. La planimétrie en forme de "L" reprend l'idée du patio, mais en s'ouvrant sur un de ses côtés de manière à élargir ses limites. Du point de vue des formes, le bâtiment est basé sur une composition de lignes, plans et cubes qui rappellent les œuvres néoplasticistes du début du vingtième siècle.

In den Werken dieses Architekten spiegelt sich auf der einen Seite die Bedeutung des Bezugs der Gebäude zu ihrem Standort und auf der anderen Seite die verschiedenen Einflüsse wider, angefangen bei der regionalen Architektur mit ihren Elementen bis hin zur modernen Architektur mit ihren formellen Ausdrucksweisen. Bei der Errichtung dieses Hauses wird ein starker Bezug zur Umgebung gebildet, in der sich zahlreiche in der Region typische Bäume befinden. Diese Vorzüge des Standortes werden bei der Planung berücksichtigt. Durch die in einer L-Form angeordnete Planimetrie lebt das Konzept des Innenhofes wieder auf, obwohl sich in diesem Fall eine Seite nach außen hin geöffnet ist, um die Grenzen zu erweitern. Die formelle Planung basiert auf einer Anordnung von Linien, Flächen und Körpern, die an die neoplastizistischen Werke im ersten Drittel des 20. Jahrhunderts erinnert.

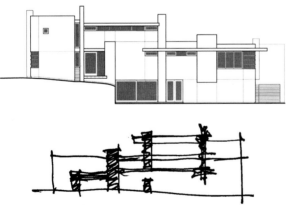

The perfect balance between the different elements of the composition confers an expressive beauty upon the design as a whole. Architecturally, each of these pieces –lines, planes and cubes– is converted into spaces.

L'équilibre entre les différents éléments de l'œuvre donne une plastique élégante à l'ensemble. Chacun d'entre eux – lignes, plans et cubes – forment les différentes pièces de la maison.

Durch das Gleichgewicht zwischen den verschiedenen Elementen des Werkes entsteht eine stilvolle räumliche Anordnung. In architektonischer Hinsicht wird jedes einzelne Element, Linien, Flächen oder Körper, zu einem Bereich.

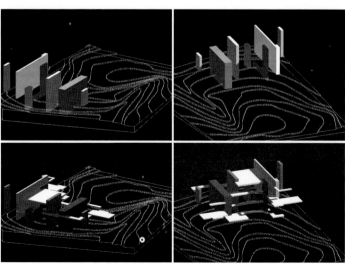

The placement of each of the rooms within the ensemble turns them into elements which generate tensions and balance within the area, apart from their formal and architectural force.

L'emplacement des différents éléments à l'intérieur du bâtiment, au-delà de leur potentiel formel et architectural, crée tensions et équilibres dans la maison.

Durch die Anordnung jedes Elements im Gesamtwerk kommt nicht nur die formelle und architektonische Kraft zum Ausdruck, sondern es werden auch Spannungen und Gleichgewicht zum Standort hergestellt.

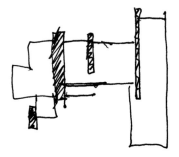

CANYON RESIDENCE

CASA CASADEVALL

ARTIGUES & SANABRIA

Barcelona, España. 1990-1991

In many cases the shape of the plot determines the geometry which must be adopted by the proposal for the building to be constructed, as for example in the case of *Casadevall House*, whose architecture was determined by the elongated dimensions of the plot. Thus the proposal was developed along a longitudinal axis, to which different elements which occasionally alter the basic line are subsequently attached. The plan thus succeeds in developing a spatial sequence in more than one direction. Formally, a low element is added onto the main volume, which makes it possible to introduce spaces such as the open courtyard in the back of the house.

La forme des terrains à bâtir détermine souvent la géométrie à adopter pour la construction d'une maison, comme c'est le cas de la casa Casadevall, où l'architecture naît des proportions élargies du terrain. Le bâtiment se développe à partir d'un axe longitudinal auquel viennent s'ajouter des éléments qui créent des alternances dans la direction suivie, ce qui permet une orientation variée de la séquence spatiale. Au niveau des formes, un élément bas vient s'ajouter au volume principal, permettant d'y intégrer des espaces supplémentaires comme le patio ouvert à l'arrière.

In vielen Fällen wird durch die Form des Grundstücks bestimmt, welche geometrischen Formen das Projekt annimmt, das auf ihm gebaut wird, wie zum Beispiel das Haus *Casadevall*, bei der die Architektur von die länglichen Proportionen des Grundstücks abhängt. Die Planung des Projektes basiert also auf einer länglichen Achse, an die Elemente angeschlossen werden, durch die diese Geradlinigkeit an einigen Stellen verändert wird. Auf diese Weise wird erreicht, dass die räumliche Sequenz nicht nur in einer Richtung angeordnet ist. Was die formelle Planung betrifft, wird an einen Hauptbaukörper ein niedriges Element angeschlossen, wodurch die Einbeziehung zusätzlicher Bereiche ermöglicht wird, wie zum Beispiel der offene Hof im hinteren Abschnitt.

The floor plan of the house was developed along a longitudinal axis which follows the direction of the plot. Thus it was possible to provide two different entrances.

Le plan de la maison se développe à partir d'un axe longitudinal qui suit la direction du terrain, permettant ainsi deux accès distincts.

Der Grundriss des Hauses wurde basierend auf einer länglichen Achse entworfen, deren Richtung der des Grundstückes entspricht. Auf diese Art werden zwei verschiedene Zugänge geschaffen.

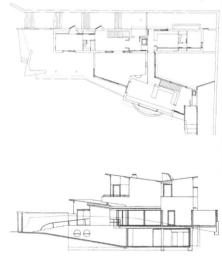

CASA CASADEVALL

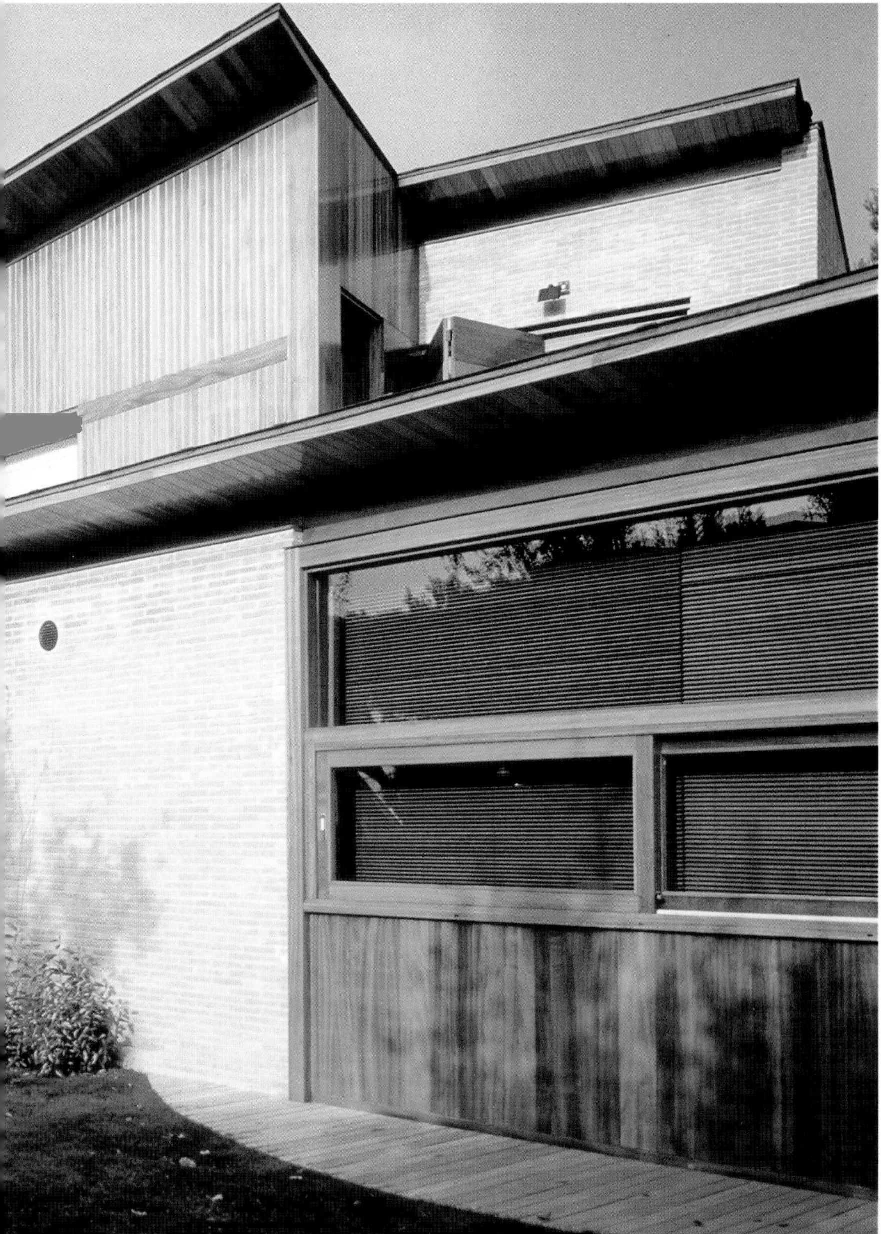

Casa CH

Baas Arquitectes. Jordi Badía, Mercè Sangenís

La Garriga, España. 2001

The team of Baas Architects, founded by Jordi Badía in 1994, received the commission for the construction of this residence, winner of the FAD 2002 awards. The expected use of the house determined the proposal of two distinct areas: the children's area on one side (destined only for occasional occupation) and on the other, that of the parents. The two areas are joined by a courtyard which acts as the structural element differentiating these spaces. While a blank wall closes the volume up on the side facing the neighbouring residences, the treatment of the approach towards the garden converts it into a frame protecting the glazed façades. In this manner the façades of the volume are separated from the partition walls. This design produces depths and hollows which create a compelling play of shadows within the dwelling.

La construction de cette maison, premier prix du FAD 2002, a été confiée à l'équipe de Baas Arquitectes, fondée par Jordi Badía en 1994. L'utilisation de la maison détermine la conception de deux zones distinctes : d'un côté, celles pour les enfants (à occupation éventuelle) et de l'autre, la partie destinée aux parents. Ces deux zones sont reliées par un patio, élément structurel de différentiation spatiale. Un volume blanc se ferme aux maisons attenantes et se transforme en un espace qui protège les façades vitrées. Ainsi les façades du volume se détachent de celles des séparations spatiales. On obtient de cette manière des profondeurs qui donnent un intéressant jeu d'ombres à l'ensemble.

Das im Jahre 1994 von Jordi Badía gegründete Team von Baas Arquitectes wurde für die Errichtung dieses Wohnhauses beauftragt, Preisträger der FAD-Auszeichnungen 2002. Die Planung zwei unterschiedlicher Bereiche basiert auf der Nutzung des Hauses. Ein Bereich wurde für die Eltern geschaffen und ein zweiter nur gelegentlich bewohnter Bereich für die Kinder. Beide Bereiche werden durch einen Innenhof verbunden, der auch gleichzeitig als strukturelles Element zur räumlichen Abgrenzung dient. Während ein weißer Baukörper komplett von den umgebenden Wohnhäusern abgeschlossen ist, wird dieser zum Garten hin zu einem Rahmen, durch den die Glasfassaden geschützt werden. Somit werden die Fassaden des Baukörpers unabhängig von den räumlichen Begrenzungen geschaffen. Aus diese Weise wird dem Gesamtwerk Tiefe und stilvolle Licht-Schatten-Effekte verliehen.

Casa CH

Casa CH

The volume of the studio stands out within the formal treatment of the residence. This treatment converts the studio into the area with one of the most exceptional views in the house.

Le volume du studio est mis en valeur à l'intérieur du traitement formel de la demeure, ce qui lui confère les vues les plus privilégiées de la maison.

Der Bereich im Dachgeschoss sticht aus der formellen Gestaltung des Wohnhauses hervor. Durch sein Design wird dieser Raum er zu dem Bereich des Hauses mit den herrlichsten Aussichten.

CASA CH

CASA CH

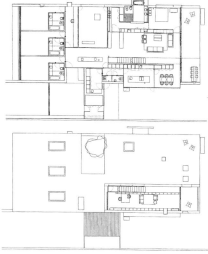

The opening up of the residence towards the garden turns this entryway, on a formal level, into an independent frame protecting the glazed walls through the creation of deep shadows.

En s'ouvrant sur le jardin, le volume devient une partie indépendante qui protège les surfaces vitrées en projetant de grandes ombres.

Durch die Öffnung des Wohnhauses zum Garten hin wird der Baukörper formell zu einem unabhängigen Rahmen, durch den Schatten entstehen, die die Glasflächen schützen.

CASA CH

CASA CORDOVA

LEGORRETA + LEGORRETA

México DF, México. 2000

Although in theory all dwellings satisfy the same basic needs for a living space, the solutions offered vary considerably according to the situation of the project. In this manner, a house located in the city –more vulnerable where the matter of privacy is concerned– must protect itself to a greater extent than a house isolated in the countryside. Thus we find that this residence in Mexico City, due to its proximity to a commercial district, closes itself off completely towards the exterior while dedicating all of its attention towards the interior. This "introversion" is reinforced by a perimeter ring with intermediate spacing which serves as a transition between the exterior and interior.

Bien que, du point de vue conceptuel, tous les logements essaient de pourvoir aux mêmes nécessités basiques, les solutions varient sensiblement selon l'emplacement du projet. Ainsi, une maison située en ville a tendance à être plus vulnérable quant à son intimité, et doit donc être davantage protégée qu'une maison isolée dans la campagne. On observe que cette habitation, proche d'une zone commerciale à Mexico, se referme complètement sur l'extérieur et se retranche vers l'intérieur. Cette "introversion" est consolidée par un anneau périphérique dont les espaces intermédiaires servent de transition entre l'intérieur et l'extérieur.

Obwohl bei der Gestaltung jeder Wohnung versucht wird, den Grundbedürfnissen der Wohnräume nachzukommen, variieren die Lösungen doch stark je nach Standort des Projektes. Demnach sollte ein Haus in der Stadt, wo die Privatsphäre gefährdeter sein kann, stärker geschützt werden als ein abgelegenes Haus in ländlicher Umgebung. Ein Beweis hierfür ist dieses Wohnhaus in Mexiko City, das wegen seiner Nähe zur Einkaufszone komplett von der Umgebung abgeschlossen ist und sich vollkommen auf das Innere bezieht. Diese "Verschlossenheit" wird zusätzlich durch einen das Gebäude umgebenden Ring verstärkt. Somit werden Zwischenräume geschaffen, die als Übergang zwischen dem Innenraum und der äußeren Umgebung wirken.

The openings towards the exterior were studied to meet the needs of the interior spaces. Thus, each of the walls for the façade of the house was designed individually, which results in an interesting play between open spaces and solid areas.

Les ouvertures sur l'extérieur sont étudiées en fonction des besoins des espaces intérieurs. Ainsi, chacun des plans de façade de la maison fonctionne individuellement, ce qui donne un intéressant mélange de creux et de solides.

Die Öffnungen nach außen variieren je nach Bedarf der Innenräume. So werden die Fassaden des Gebäudes nach individuellen Plänen entworfen, wodurch die spielerische Anordnung von Freiraum und Konstruktion zum Ausdruck kommt.

CASA CORDOVA

CASA CORDOVA

CASA EN LA COSTA MEDITERRÁNEA

MAP ARQUITECTOS. JOSEP LLUÍS MATEO

Mallorca, España. 1997 / 2000-2001

The structure of this single-family dwelling situated in the St. Pere Colony (Artà) is based on two solid pieces, with enormous chromatic contrast between them, which provide order to the main areas of the project. Once the formal image is achieved, the treatment of the façades is accomplished through delicate texture designs and walls with large glass openings. The glazed borders on the ground floor produce an effect whereby, from a certain perspective, the two main pieces appear to be "floating" which generates an interesting play of contrasts between the solidity of the structures and the lightness in their manner of resting upon the terrain.

La volumétrie de cette demeure individuelle, située dans la colonie de St. Pere (Artà), est fondée sur deux pièces maîtresses qui constituent les espaces principaux de ce projet, qu'un grand contraste chromatique fait ressortir. Une fois le traitement des formes achevé, la façade est édifiée à travers un travail délicat de textures et de plans avec de grandes baies vitrées. Les bandes de verre situées au rez-de-chaussée sont organisées de telle sorte que, d'une certaine perspective, les deux éléments dominants semblent "flotter", créant ainsi un intéressant jeu de contrastes entre la solidité des volumes et la légèreté dans leur manière de prendre appui sur le terrain.

Die Volumetrie dieses Einfamilienhauses in der Kolonie von St. Pere (Artà) basiert auf zwei Hauptabschnitten, die durch ihre farbliche Strukturierung chromatisch stark zueinander kontrastieren. Nach dem Entwurf eines formellen Bildes werden die Fassaden durch eine ausgefeilte Bearbeitung der Strukturen und Flächen mit großen Glasöffnungen gestaltet. Durch die verglaste Umrandung im Erdgeschoss werden die Hauptabschnitte aus bestimmten Perspektiven wahrgenommen, als würden sie "schwimmen". Dadurch wiederum entsteht ein interessantes Kontrastspiel zwischen der Beständigkeit der Baukörper und der Leichtigkeit der Form, in der sie sich auf das Gelände stützen.

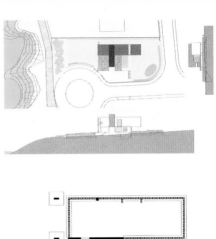

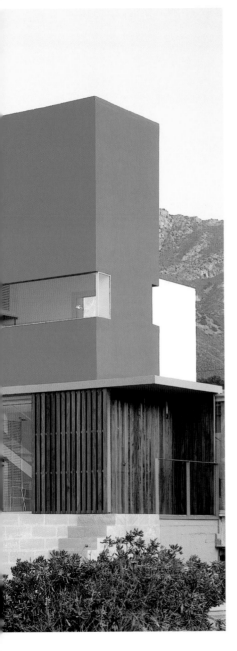

For this project the climatic conditions in the area demanded a study of systems for protecting against the wind and the heat. For this reason a courtyard is designed with its own microclimate which makes it possible to control the internal temperature in the different areas of the home.

Les conditions climatiques rendent nécessaire l'étude de systèmes de protection contre le vent et la chaleur. Un patio avec microclimat permet de contrôler la température intérieure des différentes pièces qui constituent la maison.

Durch die klimatischen Bedingungen des Standortes mussten bei der Entwicklung des Projektes die Schutzsysteme gegen den Wind und die Hitze studiert werden. Dementsprechend wurde ein Innenhof mit einem Mikroklima entworfen, wodurch die Temperatur der Innenräume des Hauses reguliert werden kann.

CASA EN LA COSTA MEDITERRÁNEA

The handling of the façades is based upon delicate texture designs and walls with large glass openings. Consequently the volumes are transformed into elements projecting transparencies, reflections and shadows.

Le traitement des façades est basé sur un travail délicat de textures et de plans avec de grandes baies vitrées. Ainsi, les volumes deviennent des éléments qui projettent transparences, reflets et ombres.

Die Gestaltung der Fassaden basiert auf einer ausgefeilten Verarbeitung der Strukturen und Flächen mit großen verglasten Öffnungen. Daher werden die Baukörper zu Elementen, durch die Transparenz, Reflexe und Schatten projiziert werden.

COTTESLOE RESIDENCE

CRAIG STEERE ARCHITECTS

Cottesloe, Australia. 2000

For this project, the architect admitted to working with concepts of a minimalist nature in order to construct a "contemporary" house. Two simple elements were proposed for the floor plan of the project: a rectangle and a square. Nonetheless, a more dynamic structure was achieved through the introduction of small variations in these shapes. On a formal level the two shapes become the main elements; a contrast was created between them by inclining the rooftop: while the area with the flat roof became a cube, the remaining element was designed with a sloping roof decorated with large eaves.

Dans ce projet, l'architecte reconnaît travailler avec des concepts de nature minimaliste dans le but de construire une "maison contemporaine". Le plan de la maison comporte deux éléments simples : un rectangle et un carré. Néanmoins, avec l'introduction de légères variations dans cette géométrie, il parvient à créer une volumétrie dynamique. Les formes représentent ici les éléments principaux. L'inclinaison des toits crée un contraste entre celles-ci : dans un de ces éléments, un toit plat devient un cube, alors que l'autre est conçu comme un plan incliné avec de grands avant-toits.

Der Architekt dieses Projektes gibt zu, minimalistische Konzepte eingesetzt zu haben, um ein "zeitgenössisches Haus" zu schaffen. Der Grundriss des Hauses besteht aus zwei einfachen Elementen, einem Rechteck und einem Quadrat. Durch den Einsatz kleiner Abwandlungen dieser geometrischen Formen wird eine größere Dynamik in der Volumetrie erzeugt. In formeller Hinsicht werden diese beiden Formen zu den Hauptelementen. Der Kontrast zwischen ihnen entsteht durch die Neigung der Dächer. Während der Baukörper mit dem flachen Dach zu einem Würfel wird, besticht das Design des zweiten durch ein geneigtes Dach mit großen Flügeln.

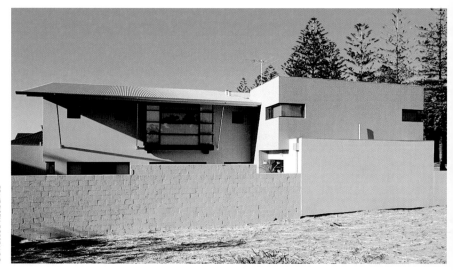

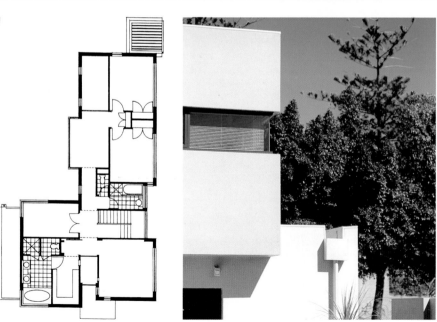

COTTESLOE RESIDENCE

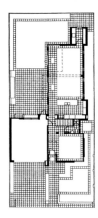

The spatial treatment was based on the characteristics of the terrain. The introduction of natural light and cross ventilation guarantee the optimum conditions of this residence oriented towards the north.

Le traitement spatial est basé sur les caractéristiques du terrain. Suivant la direction nord, l'éclairage naturel et l'aération croisée garantissent les meilleures conditions de vie dans la maison.

Die räumliche Anordnung wird durch die Beschaffenheit des Geländes bestimmt. Da das Wohnhaus nach Norden hin ausgerichtet ist, wird eine natürliche Beleuchtung und Lüftung gewährleistet, wodurch optimale Bedingungen entstehen.

COTTESLOE RESIDENCE

CUTLER RESIDENCE

MURDOCK YOUNG ARCHITECTS

New York, USA. 2002

This plot situated on a crag with an attractive 280° panorama overlooking the area, inspired a proposal for a residence which would make the most of its privileged setting right from the very beginning. With this idea in mind, the designers "spread out" the different spaces of the home over the plot using platforms pointing in different directions. These platforms serve to extend the spaces initially contained within the building towards the exterior. Thus, an attractive contrast is produced between the entrance level and the ground floor: although the former presents clearly defined boundaries between each of its spaces, the latter is characterized by platforms and glazed walls which blur these boundaries in order to create greater fluidity between the exterior and the interior.

Ce terrain vague sur un rocher escarpé, avec de magnifiques vues de 280° sur le site, dictait depuis le début un logement qui permettrait de profiter le plus possible de sa situation privilégiée. A partir de là, les auteurs "éparpillent" les espaces dans différentes directions au moyen de plates-formes qui élargissent vers l'extérieur les pièces initialement comprises dans la maison, ce qui crée un élégant contraste entre le niveau d'accès et le rez-de-chaussée. Les limites entre chaque pièce sont nettement définies à l'étage, alors qu'en bas, les plates-formes et les vitrages estompent ces limites pour apporter une plus grande fluidité entre l'intérieur et l'extérieur.

Dieses Grundstück auf einem steilen Felsen mit wunderschönen Aussichten in einem Umkreis von 280° über die Umgebung ist ideal für die Planung eines Wohnhauses, von dem aus die Vorteile des einzigartigen Standortes maximal genutzt werden können. Davon ausgehend wurden die Bereiche über den Standort "verstreut" angeordnet. Durch auf verschiedene Richtungen ausgerichtete Plattformen werden die Bereiche, die zunächst durch das Haus zusammengehalten werden, nach außen erweitert. Auf diese Weise wird ein angenehmer Kontrast zwischen der Etage mit dem Eingangsbereich und dem Erdgeschoss geschaffen. Während in der zuerst genannten die einzelnen Bereiche klar abgegrenzt sind, werden diese Grenzen im Erdgeschoss durch die Plattformen und die verglasten Flächen aufgelöst, um einen fließenden Übergang von außen nach innen zu schaffen.

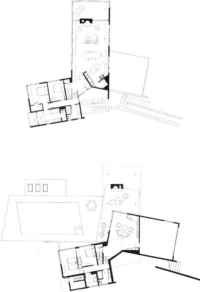

The proposal for materials is based primarily on the use of cedar wood, concrete and stone combined with glazed walls.

Les principaux matériaux utilisés pour ce projet sont le bois de cèdre, le béton et la pierre, qui se combinent avec des séparations de verre.

Die Planung der verwendeten Materialien basiert hauptsächlich auf dem Einsatz von Zedernholz, Beton und Stein, die teilweise verglast sind.

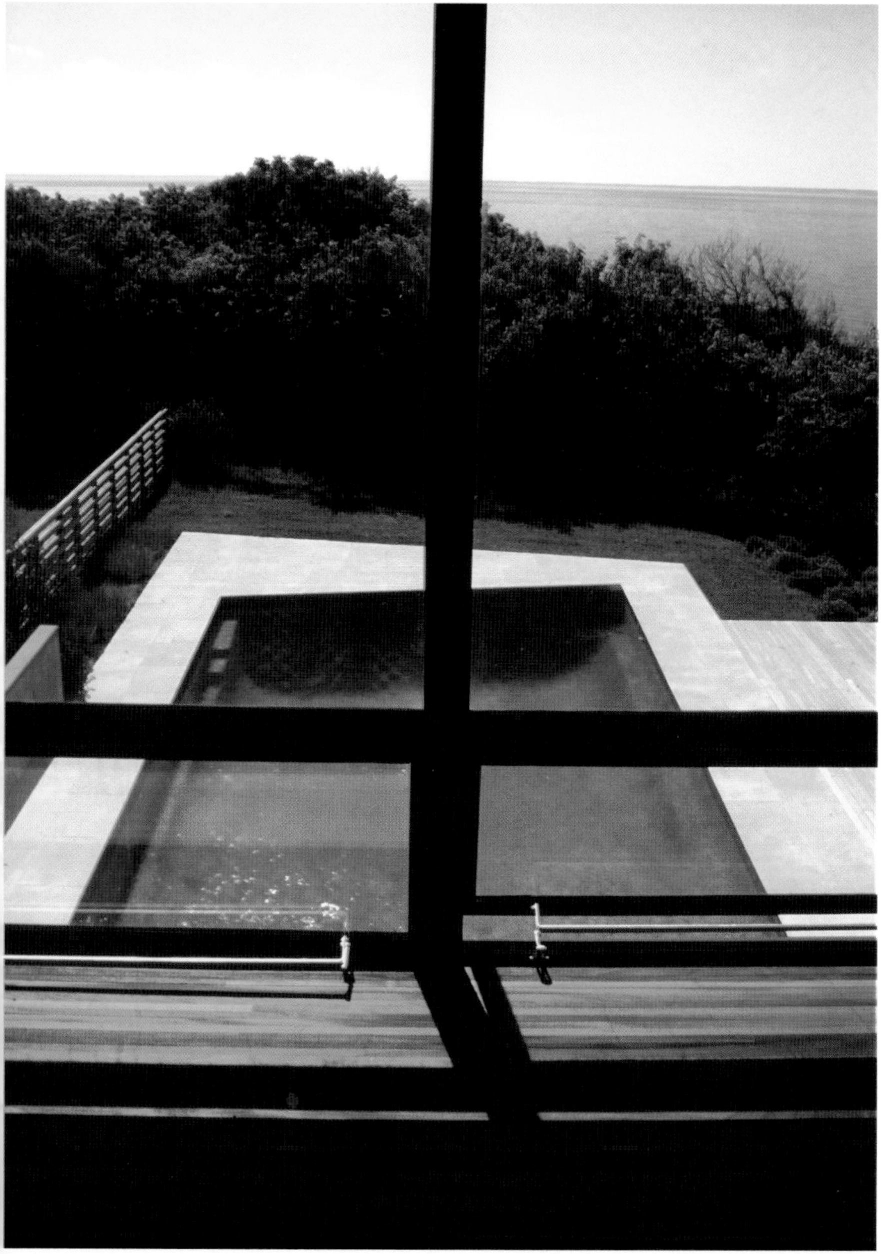

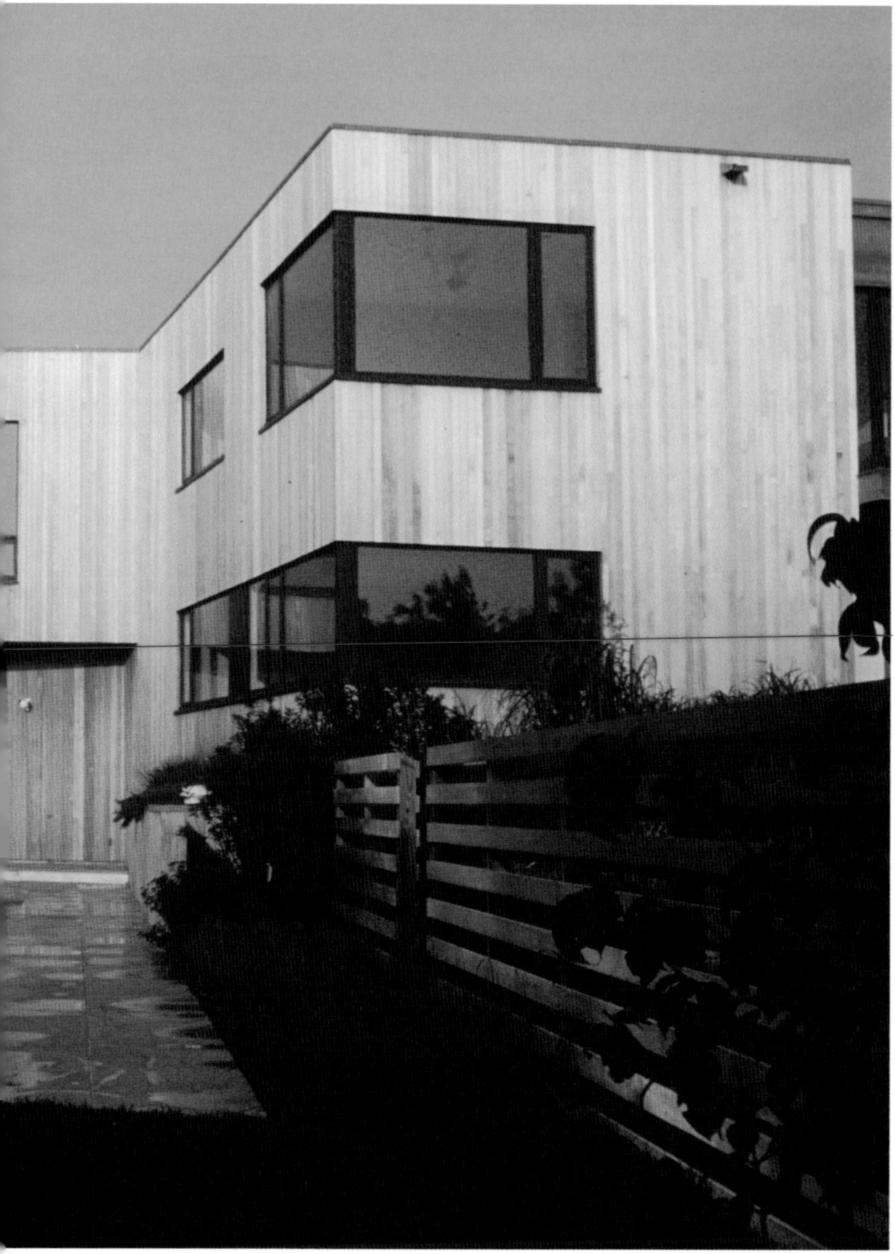

Cutler Residence

WOHNHAUS FLACHS

ERNST GISELBRECHT ARCHITEKT

Graz, Österreich. 1997-2000 / 2001

The work of Ernst Giselbrecht, one of the most outstanding figures in the new Austrian architecture, is characterized by the use of "rationalist" logic, both on a constructive as well as a formal level. A dual conception was presented in the project for this house: on the one hand, the house opens up to its surroundings by recovering the concept of a courtyard. On the other hand, a great wall closes in and completely protects the privacy of the home. This dual condition is also reflected in the use of materials: large glazed walls extend the interior spaces towards the courtyard, while the use of colour reinforces the presence of the solid wall.

L'œuvre d'Ernst Giselbrecht, une des figures les plus importantes de l'architecture contemporaine autrichienne, se distingue par l'utilisation logique "rationaliste", tant au niveau de la construction que des formes. Une double conception est présente dans ce projet. Si d'un côté le bâtiment s'ouvre sur l'extérieur en reprenant l'idée du patio, d'un autre côté, un grand mur renferme et protège entièrement l'intimité de la maison. Les matériaux utilisés reflètent eux aussi cette double condition : de grandes surfaces vitrées prolongent les espaces intérieurs vers le patio, tandis que la présence de ce mur épais est renforcée par la couleur utilisée.

Das Werk von Ernst Giselbrecht, einem der bedeutendsten Architekten Österreichs, zeichnet sich durch Logik und "Vernunft" aus, was sowohl in der Bauweise als auch in der formellen Anordnung zum Ausdruck kommt. Der Entwurf dieses Hauses sieht zwei verschiedene Blickwinkel vor. Auf der einen Seite wird das Haus durch den Hof der Umgebung geöffnet, während es auf der anderen Seite durch eine hohe Mauer komplett verschlossen und die Privatsphäre der Bewohner bewahrt wird. Diese zwei Blickwinkel werden auch im Einsatz der Materialien deutlich. Auf der Seite, die zum Hof zeigt, werden die Innenräume durch große Glasflächen erweitert, während die Beständigkeit der Mauer durch den farblichen Einsatz noch verstärkt wird.

The planimetry suggests the course for the development of the project right from the very beginning: while the spaces open up towards the interior, the exterior lines which mark the boundaries of the house are reinforced by a wall.

La planimétrie suggère dès le début du projet le chemin à prendre. Alors que les divers espaces s'ouvrent vers l'intérieur, un mur vient renforcer les lignes extérieures qui délimitent la maison.

In der Planimetrie wird die Projektentwicklung von Anfang an festgelegt. Während die Bereiche zum Hof geöffnet sind, werden die Linien, durch die das Haus nach außen hin abgegrenzt wird, durch eine Mauer verstärkt.

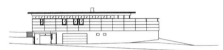

The dual posture of the project is demonstrated by the different treatments applied to the façades: on the one hand the house opens up towards the garden using glazed partitions, while on the other hand it closes itself up completely behind a solid wall.

La double position du projet est mise en évidence par la différence dans le traitement des façades : d'un côté la maison s'ouvre sur le jardin à travers des vitrages, alors que de l'autre elle se ferme complètement au moyen d'un grand mur.

Die zwei verschiedenen Blickwinkel, nach denen das Projekt entwickelt wurde, spiegeln sich auch in der unterschiedlichen Gestaltung der Fassaden wider. Auf der einen Seite wird durch die Glasflächen zum Garten hin die Transparenz unterstrichen, während das Haus auf der anderen Seite durch eine hohe Mauer komplett nach außen hin geschlossen ist.

WOHNHAUS FLACHS

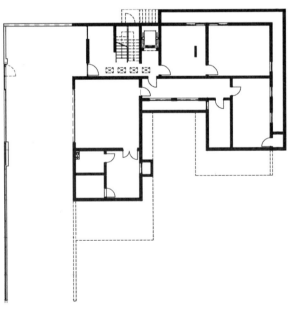

RESIDENTIAL HOUSE FLATZ

B & E BAUMSCHLAGER-EBERLE

Schaan, Liechtenstein. 1998 / 1999-2000

An elegant ensemble of cubic concrete volumes lends the image to this single-family dwelling in the suburbs of the community of Schaan, in the Principality of Liechtenstein. Making the most of the beauty of the area was the main consideration for the positioning of this structure within the plot and its spatial organization. The austerity of its formal treatment and the use of concrete in its natural shade endow the house with a notable sculptural image. The control of the materials and their colour reinforce the delicacy of the project: concrete with yellow pigmentation on the outside and interiors of white plaster, wood and green-tinged stone complete the effect.

Un élégant ensemble de volumes cubiques en béton donne forme à ce logement individuel des environs de la communauté de Schaan, dans la principauté du Liechtenstein. Mettre en valeur les attraits de ce site fut le critère décisif au choix de son emplacement sur le terrain et de son organisation spatiale. L'austérité des formes et l'utilisation du béton dans sa couleur naturelle donnent une image sculpturale accentuée à la résidence. Le contrôle des matériaux et de leur couleur fait ressortir la délicatesse du projet ; béton pigmenté de jaune devant la maison, intérieurs de plâtre blanc, bois et pierre verdâtre le complètent.

Eine elegante Kombination kubischer Baukörper aus Beton bestimmen das Bild dieses Einfamilienhauses am Stadtrand der Gemeinde Schaan im Fürstentum Liechtenstein. Das gänzliche Ausschöpfen der Vorzüge des Standortes war das Hauptkriterium für die Positionierung der Volumetrie auf dem Grundstück und seine räumliche Anordnung. Die formelle Strenge und der Einsatz von Beton in seiner natürlichen Farbe verleihen dem Haus einen markanten skulpturellen Eindruck. Die Strenge der Materialien und ihrer Farben verstärken die Feinheit des Projektes. Das Äußere besticht durch gelb getönten Beton, die Innenräume durch weiße Anstriche. Das Ganze wird durch Holz und grünliche Steine verziert.

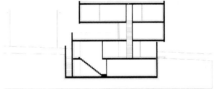

In the distance the Rhine Valley is visible to the Swiss mountains. This privileged view is well-exploited on the upper floor. Nonetheless, generous openings in the façade provide the opportunity to enjoy this view from the lower levels as well.

On distingue au loin la vallée du Rhin qui rejoint les montagnes suisses. Cette vue privilégiée est intensifiée du dernier étage, mais de grandes ouvertures sur les façades permettent aussi de l'admirer depuis les niveaux inférieurs.

In der Ferne kann man vom Rheintal bis zu den Schweizer Bergen sehen. Diese einzigartige Aussicht wird im Obergeschoss vollkommen ausgeschöpft. Jedoch wird durch die großen Öffnungen in den Fassaden sein Genuss auch von den unteren Geschossen aus ermöglicht.

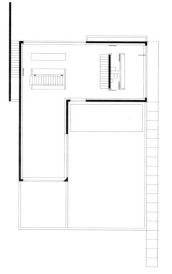

This project, 227 m². of constructed area, was developed on the basis of a structure with orthogonal lines. The bedrooms were planned on two distinct levels: on the first floor we find the parents' chamber and on the second, that of the children.

Ce projet de construction de 227 m² est basé sur une volumétrie de lignes orthogonales. Les chambres sont implantées à deux niveaux : le premier étage pour les parents et le deuxième pour les enfants.

Das Projekt mit einer bebauten Oberfläche von 227 m² besteht aus einer Volumetrie orthogonaler Linien. Die Zimmer teilen sich auf zwei verschiedene Etagen auf. Im ersten Geschoß befindet sich das Schlafzimmer und im zweiten das Kinderzimmer.

FURNITURE HOUSE 1

SHIGERU BAN

Yamanaka, Japan. 1995

The design of this house in the mountains of Yamanaka is based on respect towards the characteristics of the natural surroundings through the use of a given constructive system. In order to accelerate the construction process, prefabricated "furniture units" which guaranteed quality control during construction were used; this also lead to a reduction in costs. In addition to the constructive virtues of these elements, they also played a role in determining the measurements of the project structurally and spatially. The 2,4 m. high elements display different widths according to their uses: from a width of 0,90 m. for the storage areas to 0,45 m. on bookcases and shelves.

Le concept de cette maison, dans les montagnes de Yamanaka, est fondé sur le respect des conditions environnementales naturelles, grâce au recours à un système constructif particulier. Des "unités mobilières" préfabriquées ont été utilisées afin de faciliter la procédure de mise en œuvre, garantissant le contrôle de la qualité du projet tout en réduisant les coûts. En plus de leurs vertus constructives, ces éléments opèrent à niveau structurel et spatial, déterminant les dimensions du projet. De 2,4 m de hauteur, leur largeur varie selon leur usage : de 0,90 m pour les espaces d'entreposage à 0,45 m pour la bibliothèque et les étagères.

Die Gestaltung dieses Hauses in den Bergen von Yamanaka basiert auf dem Respekt der Beschaffenheit der natürlichen Umgebung gegenüber, der sich im angewandten Bausystem widerspiegelt. Das Haus wurde durch vorgefertigte Elemente eingerichtet, um den Bauprozess zu beschleunigen. Dadurch wurden gleichzeitig die Qualitätskontrolle beim Bau garantiert und die Kosten gesenkt. Durch diese Elemente wird nicht nur der Bau erleichtert sondern auch die Struktur und räumliche Ausdehnung der Dimensionen des Projektes bestimmt. Die Breite der Elemente mit einer Höhe von 2,4 m ist variabel, je nach Einsatz. Sie variieren von 0,90 m für Lagerräume bis zu 0,45 m für Büchereien und Regale.

Various furniture units are used as the elements defining the different areas within a single space.

Les différentes unités mobilières agissent comme des éléments qui définissent divers milieux au sein d'un même espace.

Durch den Einsatz der verschiedenen Elemente wurden die unterschiedlichen Räume in einem Bereich abgegrenzt.

Furniture House 1

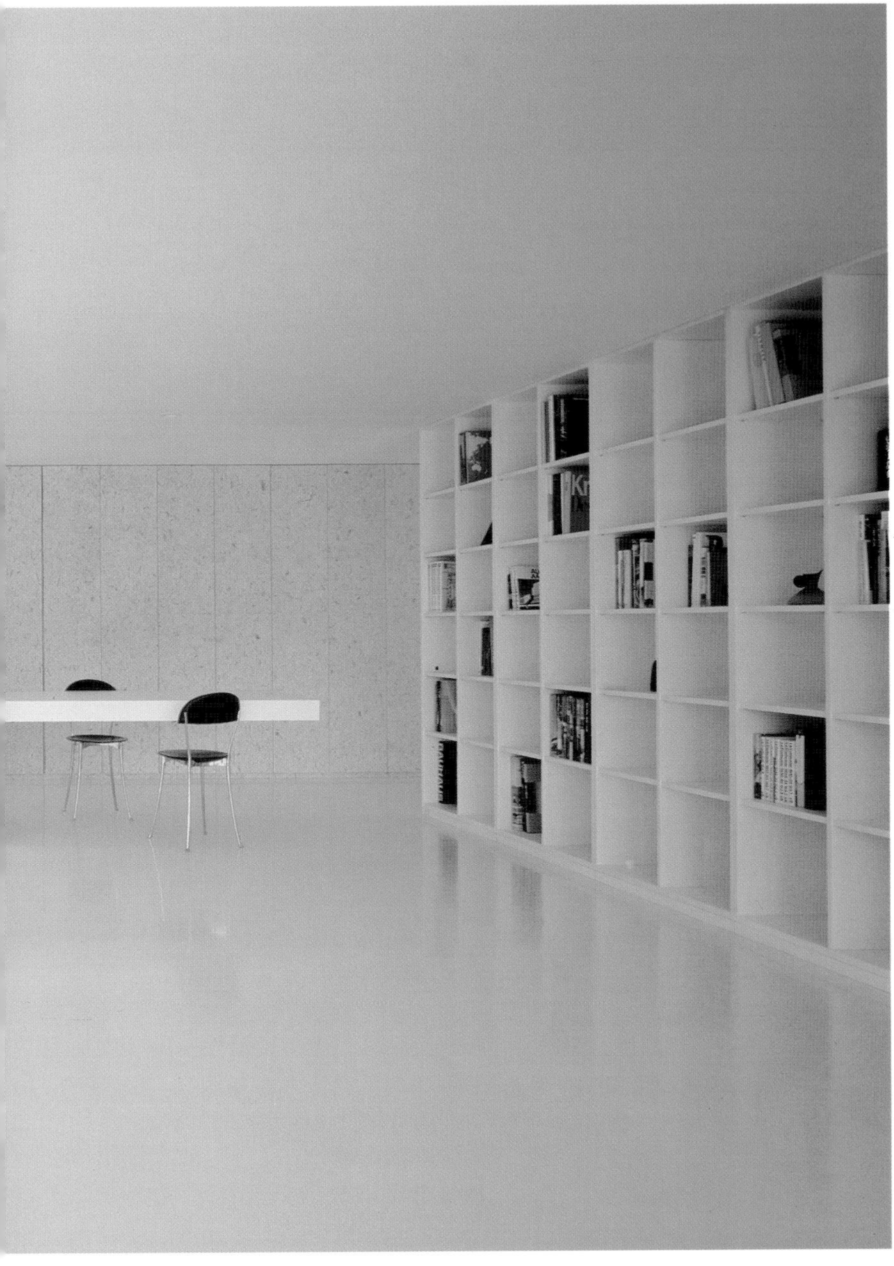

NEW HOUSE IN GALWAY

MARK GUARD ARCHITECTS

Galway, Ireland. 1992

The situation of this house in a non-urban environment allowed for the proposal of a project deeply rooted in the tradition of rural Irish homes. Although its simplicity is one of the primary virtues of the project, the possibility of innovative proposals, either on a formal or spatial level, was not forgotten. Hence, a design with an unusual arrangement was created: on the one hand, a part of the private spaces –the children's bedrooms– was placed on the ground floor allowing them direct access to the garden. On the other hand, the living-room on the upper floor enjoys the virtues of natural sunlight, the full height of the ceiling and the views over the location.

L'emplacement de cette maison dans un environnement non urbain offre la possibilité d'un projet qui embrasse la tradition des maisons rurales irlandaises. Bien que la simplicité soit l'un des principaux atouts de ce projet, l'hypothèse d'une construction novatrice, que ce soit au niveau des formes ou de l'espace, n'a pas été négligée. Ainsi, nous nous trouvons face à une organisation du bâtiment peu fréquente : d'une part, certains des espaces privés, en l'occurrence les chambres des enfants, se situent au rez-de-chaussée, en contact direct avec le jardin ; d'autre part, le salon à l'étage permet d'exploiter les vertus de la lumière naturelle, la hauteur des toits et les vues sur le paysage environnant.

Die Lage dieses Hauses in einem ländlichen Umfeld ermöglichte die Planung eines Projektes, das fest mit der Tradition der ländlichen Wohnhäuser Irlands verwurzelt ist. Obgleich die Einfachheit einer der größten Vorzüge des Projektes ist, werden auch die Möglichkeiten moderner formeller und räumlicher Planungen in Betracht gezogen. Dadurch entsteht eine etwas unkonventionelle Anordnung des Programmes. Auf der einen Seite befinden sich die zum privaten Bereich gehörenden Kinderzimmer im Erdgeschoss, wo sie einen direkten Bezug zum Garten erhalten. Auf der anderen Seite werden im auf der oberen Etage angeordneten Wohnzimmer die Vorteile des natürlichen Lichtes, die Deckenhöhe und die Ausblicke über die Umgebung genossen.

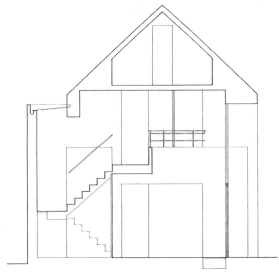

This house is located in a rural setting in the outskirts of the city of Galway. The attractive views are flanked by areas of ancient trees and bushes.

Cette maison se situe dans les environs de Galway, dans un charmant quartier au caractère rural, bordé de vieux arbres et d'arbustes.

Dieses Haus befindet sich am Stadtrand von Galway in einer ländlichen Umgebung. Die herrlichen Aussichten werden durch alte Bäume und Buschwerk noch verschönt.

NEW HOUSE IN GALWAY

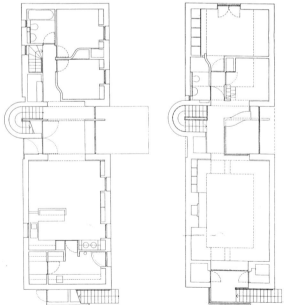

The internal arrangement possesses great versatility: through the use of sliding walls, the rooms can be enlarged or subdivided as needed. The austerity of the dwelling is enhanced, both inside and out, by the use of white.

L'organisation intérieure est très variée : des portes coulissantes agrandissent ou subdivisent les différents espaces à discrétion. L'austérité de la demeure est mise en valeur dehors comme dedans, par l'utilisation du blanc.

Die innere Anordnung ist sehr vielseitig gestaltet. Durch Schiebeflächen werden die Räume je nach Bedarf erweitert oder abgegrenzt. Die Einfachheit des Wohnhauses wird innen und außen durch weiße Farbtöne zum Ausdruck gebracht.

GREENWICH HOUSE

HARIRI & HARIRI

Connecticut, USA. 1996-1998

According to its designers, the proposal for this house was based on an investigation into the concept of the suburban residence and its relationship with the new lifestyle of its inhabitants. An L-shaped house re-using an existing structure was proposed, with a plan based entirely around two wings of the house. The meeting point between the two wings also serves as the nexus between the inhabitants and the world around them: an area with a large television screen and a telecommunications system replaces what would otherwise have been a living-room. Formally, the project revolves around an attractive experiment with lights and transparencies.

Le projet de cette maison, comme le reconnaissent ses auteurs, est fondé sur la quête d'un concept suburbain et de ses relations avec le mode de vie actuel de ses habitants. Cette maison en forme de L réutilise une structure déjà existante, avec deux ailes qui organisent le plan entier de la maison. Le point de connexion entre ces deux ailes sert de point de rattachement entre les habitants et le monde qui les entoure : une salle avec un écran de télévision géant et un équipement de télécommunication remplace ce qui aurait pu être le salon. Du point de vue des formes, le projet est basé sur une fascinante étude de lumières et de transparences.

Die Planung dieses Hauses basiert auf der Erforschung des Konzeptes eines vorstädtischen Wohnhauses und seinen Beziehungen mit der neuen Lebensweise seiner Bewohner. Eine bestehende Struktur wird wieder aufgegriffen, wodurch das Haus in einer L-Form errichtet wird, mit zwei Flügeln, aus denen das gesamte Wohnprojekt besteht. Der Verbindungspunkt, an dem sich beide Flügel treffen, ist gleichzeitig der Bereich, in dem die Bewohner zu ihrer äußeren Umgebung eine Verbindung aufbauen. Wo der Bereich für ein Wohnzimmer hätte sein können, befindet sich stattdessen ein Raum mit einem großen Fernsehbildschirm und einer Telekommunikationsanlage. Die formelle Gestaltung basiert auf einer Studie angenehmer Effekte von Licht und Transparenz.

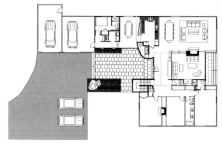

The refined treatment of the lighting in the design of this house, destined for a couple with 3 children, generates an attractive play of light, shadow and transparencies.

Le traitement raffiné de l'éclairage crée dans cette maison pour un couple et leurs trois enfants un magnifique jeu de lumières, d'ombres et de transparences.

Durch die effektive Nutzung des Lichtes in diesem Haus, in dem ein Ehepaar und drei Kinder wohnen, werden angenehme Licht-Schatten-Effekte und Transparenz erzeugt.

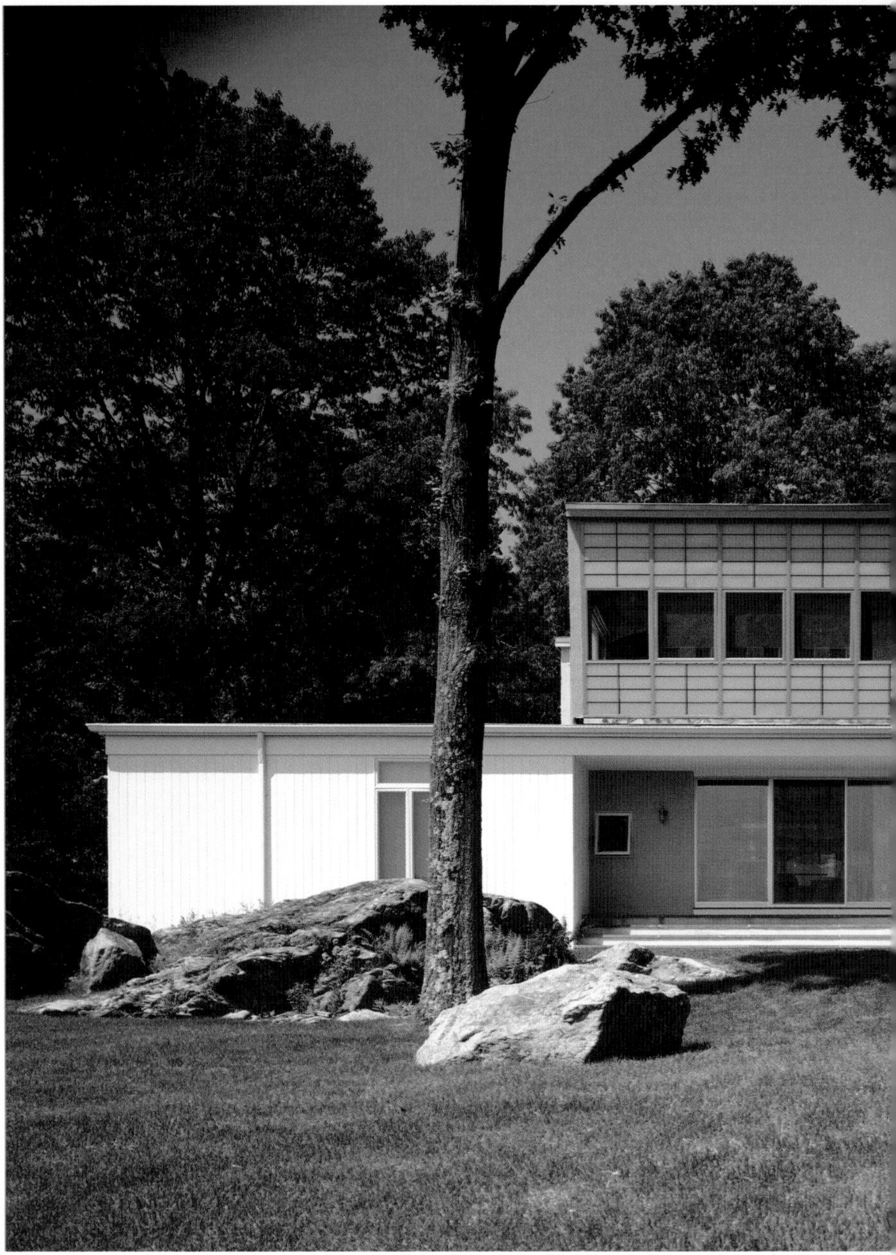

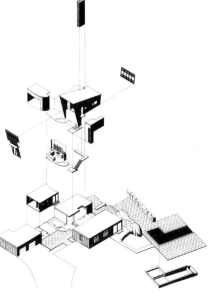

DE HELD GRONINGEN

(EEA) ERICK VAN EGERAAT ASSOCIATED ARCHITECTS

Groningen, The Netherlands. 1995-1997 /1999

Residential housing developments based on the repetition of a single unit do not necessarily imply the systematic construction of the same type of house. This dwelling located in the west end of the city of Groningen, in an area bordered by a protected forest and a mountain, belongs to a group of 67 houses. In this case the proposal for a basic structural type is conceived as a variable element within the group. The result is a floor plan with an interior courtyard as the basis for the organization of the spaces and the terraces, allowing for the possibility of introducing variations in the formal and functional treatments which would render each of the dwellings unique.

Développer des complexes résidentiels à partir d'une unité qui se répète n'implique pas nécessairement la construction systématique d'un même type de bâtiment. Cette habitation située à l'ouest de la ville de Groningen, à proximité d'un bois protégé et d'une montagne, appartient à un groupe de 67 maisons. La typologie de base de ce projet est conçue comme un élément variable à l'intérieur de l'ensemble. En conséquence, le patio intérieur organise les espaces et les terrasses de manière à introduire des variations dans le traitement formel et fonctionnel, qui rendent chacun des logements unique.

Obwohl die Erschließung von Wohnsiedlungen auf der Kopie eines Gebäudes basiert, heißt das nicht, das eine einzige Bauweise bei der Errichtung aller Häuser systematisch eingehalten wird. Dieses Wohnhaus westlich der Stadt Gröningen, befindet sich am Waldrand in der Nähe eines Gebirges und gehört zu einer Gruppe von 67 Häusern. In diesem Fall wird die Planung der grundlegenden Typologie als variables Element im Gesamtwerk angesehen. Daher werden die Bereiche und Terrassen auf einer Ebene mit dem Innenhof angeordnet, wodurch die formelle und funktionelle Gestaltung von Haus zu Haus unterschiedlich ist, wodurch jedes Wohnhaus einzigartig ist.

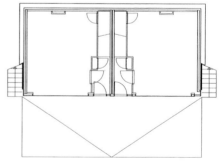

Ground floor type B.

Rez-de-chaussée de typologie B

Erdgeschoss Typologie B.

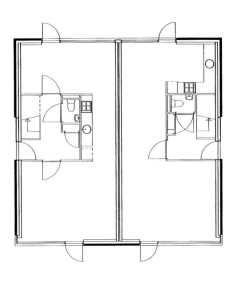

Ground floor type A.

Rez-de-chaussée de typologie A

Erdgeschoss Typologie A.

PRIVATE RESIDENCE IN HARRISON

SIDNAM PETRONE GARTNER ARCHITECTS

New York, USA. 1999-2000

These architects believe that architecture should be the product of the multiple tensions to which a project is subjected. This idea is clearly reflected in this residence located in Westchester County. The conditions of the location –a profusely wooded, rocky land with exceptionally uneven terrain– were the starting point for the project. This particular placement situation was exploited to the utmost, from the points of view of both the architects and the client, who desired a double height space overlooking the most important rock in the area. Thus, the ground plan was arranged into two wings which fit snugly between the rocks and trees, leaving an attractive double height room facing one of the most prominent rocks in the area.

L'architecture, pour ces auteurs, doit être le résultat des tensions multiples auxquelles est soumis un projet, phénomène qui se reflète clairement dans cette maison située à Westchester County. Les conditions environnantes – une région très boisée avec des rochers et de grandes dénivellations – constituent le point de départ de ce projet. Du point de vue de l'architecture, et suivant l'idée du client, qui souhaitait une structure à deux niveaux face aux rochers les plus imposants de cette zone, les caractéristiques géographiques sont exploitées au maximum. Cette habitation est répartie en deux ailes qui s'imbriquent entre les rochers et les arbres, formant une superbe composition à double hauteur faisant face à l'un des rochers les plus impressionnants alentour.

Für diese Architekten ist ihr Handwerk vermutlich das Ergebnis der vielfachen Spannungen, denen die Entwicklung eines Projektes ausgesetzt ist. Das ist bei diesem Haus mit Standort im *Westchester County* klar erkennbar. Die Beschaffenheit des stark bewaldeten und felsigen Standortes, der sich außerdem durch starke Neigungen auszeichnet, bilden den Ausgangspunkt für das Projekt. Sowohl aus architektonischer Sicht als auch aus der des Auftraggebers, auf dessen Wunsch ein Bereich auf doppelter Höhe dem bekanntesten Felsen des Standortes gegenüber angeordnet werden sollte, wird die Beschaffenheit des Standortes maximal genutzt. Der Grundriss des Gebäudes wird dementsprechend in zwei zwischen Felsen und Bäumen angeordnete Flügel aufgeteilt, wodurch ein stilvoller Bereich auf doppelter Höhe einem der bekanntesten Felsen der Umgebung gegenüber entsteht.

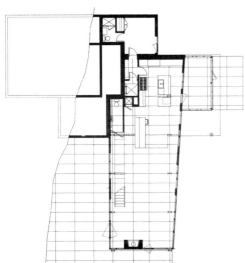

Although this project "fits in snugly" between the rocks in the area, a clear distinction exists between nature and architecture, both in terms of the type of proposal as well as in the use of materials.

Bien que cette construction "s'emboîte" dans les rochers, il existe une nette distinction entre nature et architecture, aussi bien pour le type de projet choisi que pour l'utilisation des matériaux.

Obgleich das Projekt zwischen den Felsen des Standortes angeordnet ist, wird zwischen Natur und Architektur klar unterschieden, sowohl durch die Art der Planung als auch durch den Einsatz der Materialien.

Wohnhaus Hermann

Ernst Giselbrecht Architekt

Steiermark, Österreich. 1996 / 1997

From a constructive point of view, the work of this Austrian architect includes concepts of great clarity which permit the use of technology without neglecting either the relationships between architecture and the surrounding area or the specific conditions of the commission. In this residence, the characteristics of the client, a carpenter and his family, and of the program –a house with an apartment– were decisive factors in the project. Thus a dwelling made of wood, which takes full advantage of the qualities –both constructive as well as architectural– of this material, was proposed. Spatially, the proposal of terraces is of great importance for the structuring of the program.

Du point de vue constructif, l'œuvre de cet architecte autrichien utilise des concepts de grande clarté qui permettent d'utiliser la technologie moderne sans perdre de vue les relations entre l'architecture, le paysage, et les conditions particulières de la commande. Dans cette maison, la nature du client – un menuisier et sa famille – et du programme, une maison avec appartement, déterminent le projet de manière décisive. Le résultat est une composition de bois, qui, à partir de la logique du matériel, exploite au mieux ses valeurs constructives et architecturales. Les terrasses occupent une place importante dans la structure spatiale du projet.

Bautechnisch gesehen werden in dem Werk des österreichischen Architekten sehr klare Konzepte verwendet, in die die Technologie einbezogen wird, ohne den Bezug der Architektur zum Standpunkt und die speziellen Bedingungen des Auftrages außer Acht zu lassen. Bei der Entwicklung des Projektes standen die Eigenschaften des Auftraggebers, ein Tischler und seine Familie, sowie die Art der Planung, ein Haus mit einer Wohnung, im Vordergrund. Dementsprechend wurde bei dem Bau des Wohnhauses Holz eingesetzt, ein Material, durch das sowohl die baulichen als auch die architektonischen Werte potenziert werden. Für die räumliche Einteilung ist die Planung von Terrassen von großer Bedeutung.

The planimetric proposal for the house –with orthogonal lines– made it possible to propose a central entrance which would separate the apartment from the house in a natural fashion.

La proposition planimétrique de la maison, aux lignes orthogonales, permet l'introduction d'une entrée centrale qui tient lieu de séparation naturelle avec l'emplacement destiné à l'appartement.

Der Entwurf des Grundrisses des Hauses basiert auf orthogonal angeordneten Linien und ermöglicht somit die Anordnung eines Haupteinganges, durch den auf natürliche Weise der Bereich der Wohnung abgegrenzt wird.

WOHNHAUS HERMANN

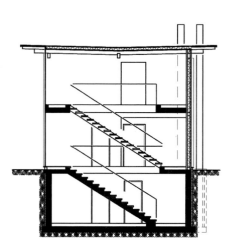

The use of wood in the front of the building contrasts with the white walls in the back.

L'utilisation du bois sur le devant de la maison crée un contraste avec les murs blancs que l'on trouve à l'arrière.

Der Einsatz von Holz an der Fassade bildet einen Kontrast zu den weißen Wänden der Hinterseite.

HOLLY BUSH HOUSE

m³ ARCHITECTS. NADI JAHANGARI, KEN HUTT, JOHN LACEY, KELLY VAN COTTEM

London, United Kingdom. 200☐

A house which has existed since 1930, located on Holly Bush Mountain to the east of London, needed to be expanded by 50% in order to fulfil the requirements of its owners, thus avoiding an otherwise inevitable change of residence. The team of m³ Architects proposes "cutting away" the back of the house, in order to make room for an attractive glazed 3-level structure. Platforms on the different levels provide greater spatial integration with the garden: one such platform at roof level generates enticing views over the garden while another on the ground floor joins the kitchen directly to the green spaces.

Il était prévu que cette maison, qui date de 1930 et qui se situe sur la montagne de Holly Bush à l'est de Londres, soit agrandie de 50% à la requête de ses propriétaires, leur évitant ainsi d'avoir à déménager. L'équipe de m³ Architects suggère alors une "coupure" dans la partie arrière de la maison, pour faire place à une magnifique structure à trois niveaux entièrement vitrée. Les plates-formes à différents niveaux favorisent une meilleure adaptation spatiale avec le jardin : la première, sur le toit, offre une très belle vue sur le jardin, et l'autre plate-forme, située au rez-de-chaussée, unit directement la cuisine et les espaces verts.

Ein Haus aus dem Jahre 1930 i☐ dem Gebirge Holly Bush östlic☐ von London sollte um 50% er☐ weitert werden, um dem Bedarf sei☐ ner Eigentümer gerecht zu werde☐ und somit deren Wechsel des Wohn☐ sitzes zu vermeiden. Das Team von m☐ Architects planen einen "Aufriss" in☐ hinteren Abschnitt des Hauses, un☐ den Weg für einen stilvollen Anba☐ mit drei vollkommen verglasten Eta☐ gen zu bahnen. Durch Plattforme☐ auf den verschiedenen Etagen wir☐ eine vorteilhaftere räumliche Abstim☐ mung auf den Garten gewährt. Vo☐ der Plattform auf der oberen Etag☐ wird eine attraktive Aussicht über de☐ Garten geboten, während eine weiter☐ im Erdgeschoss als Verbindung de☐ Küche mit der Grünanlage dient.

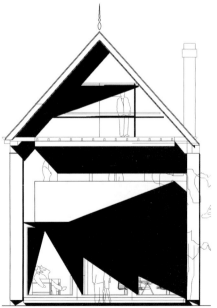

In order to carry out the expansion of the existing residence, which dates from 1930, a formal and spatial reorganization in the back of the building was proposed. Thus the project, in spite of its contrast with the existing structure, still respects the original architecture.

Afin de mener à bien l'agrandissement de cette maison vieille de plus de 70 ans, on propose une réorganisation spatiale et formelle dans la section arrière. Ce projet tranche avec le bâtiment existant tout en respectant l'architecture d'origine.

Für den Anbau an das Wohnhaus, dessen Konstruktion auf das Jahr 1930 zurückgeht, wird eine räumliche und formelle Umgestaltung des hinteren Hausabschnittes geplant. Auf diese Weise wird in dem Projekt, das mit dem bestehenden kontrastiert, trotzdem die ursprüngliche Bauweise respektiert.

HOLLY BUSH HOUSE

CASA HOWE

LEGORRETA + LEGORRETA

Reno, Nevada. USA. 1999

The forceful winds of the region imbue the setting of this house with a peculiar profile. The dwelling, surrounded only by shrubs and rocks, rises up out of the landscape almost like a monastic refuge. The composition is based on walls and towers which provide order to the spaces of the program. The walls, which mark the horizontal and linear areas in the project, suggest a boundless extension while the towers, representing the vertical aspects, are in charge of restructuring the boundaries. The position of the towers within the confines suggests the spatial variations in the interior as seen from the outside, for example by highlighting the presence of a chapel.

Les vents forts de la région donnent un caractère particulier à l'emplacement de cette maison. Entourée exclusivement d'arbustes et de roches, cette propriété se dresse tel un refuge au caractère presque monacal au milieu du paysage. La composition est basée sur le travail des murs et des tours qui gèrent l'espace alentour. Les murs, qui marquent l'aspect horizontal et linéaire du projet, suggèrent une extension sans limites, alors que les tours, qui soulignent la verticalité, ont pour fonction la restructuration de ces démarcations. La position des tours à l'intérieur de l'ensemble suggère de l'extérieur la diversité spatiale intérieure, avec par exemple la présence d'une chapelle.

Die starken Winde der Gegend verleihen dem Standort dieses Hauses einen eigentümlichen Charakter. Einem Kloster ähnlich, erhebt sich das Wohnhaus inmitten einer kargen Landschaft mit Sträuchern und Felsen wie ein Zufluchtsort. Das Design basiert auf der Arbeit mit Mauern und Türmen, durch die die räumliche Anordnung des Programmes bestimmt wird. Durch die Mauern werden dem Projekt Horizontalität und Liniarität, sowie eine Ausdehnung ohne Grenzen verliehen, während durch die Türme Vertikalität betont und diese Grenzen neu definiert werden. Die Anordnung dieser Türme im Gesamtbild lässt von außen die räumliche Vielfalt im Inneren vermuten, indem sie beispielsweise die Existenz einer Kapelle betonen.

The need to introduce natural light into all the spaces, as well as the control of this lighting, produces the variations in the openings on the façades: slots, high and low-placed windows and skylights illuminate the interior.

Le besoin de laisser passer le jour dans les différents espaces et le contrôle sur cette lumière naturelle apporte diversité aux ouvertures de la façade : fentes, fenêtres hautes et basses et vasistas illuminent l'habitation.

Es ist beabsichtigt, in allen Räumen das Sonnenlicht auszunutzen. Daher die abwechslungsreiche Anordnung der Öffnungen in den Fassaden, wie Luken, hohe und niedrige Fenster sowie Dachfenster, durch die die Innenräume ausgeleuchtet werden.

CASA HOWE

Almost all the entire residence was laid out on the ground floor which makes it possible to reinforce the idea of horizontality in the project. Thus the bedrooms are placed around a central courtyard with sculptures. The only room proposed for the second level is the master bedroom.

L'habitation s'organise presque entièrement au rez-de-chaussée, ce qui souligne l'idée d'horizontalité du projet. Les chambres entourent un patio central où l'on peut trouver diverses sculptures. Seule la chambre principale occupe l'étage.

Fast die gesamte Wohnung befindet sich im Erdgeschoss, wodurch die Horizontalität im Projekt zusätzlich betont wird. Die Zimmer umschließen einen zentralen Innenhof mit Statuen. Lediglich das Hauptzimmer befindet sich im zweiten Geschoß.

CASA HOWE

INB HOUSE

MAKI AND ASSOCIATES

Tokyo, Japan.2001

A light-coloured volume with simple orthogonal lines, divided into two parts due to the height restrictions in the area, shelters the residence of a couple and their son. Marble and aluminium have been added to concrete and glass. The intrinsic properties of these materials tend to project an image of solidity, of heaviness even, in a building; nonetheless in this case the opposite effect is achieved, with an attractive perception of lightness in all the spaces. This combined with the handling of the lighting generates an interesting spatial sequence based on the passageways and the shadows.

Une composition aux couleurs claires et aux lignes orthogonales simples qui se divise en deux pour respecter les restrictions de hauteur de la zone, abrite la demeure d'un couple et de leur fils. Au béton et au verre viennent s'ajouter le marbre et l'aluminium. Les propriétés intrinsèques de ces matériaux ont souvent tendance à projeter une image de solidité, voire de lourdeur. Cependant, c'est l'effet contraire qui a lieu ici, avec une agréable sensation de légèreté dans chacune des pièces, ce qui, uni au traitement de la lumière, produit une intéressante séquence spatiale basée sur les tracés et les ombres.

Ein Baukörper in hellen Farbtönen und mit einfachen orthogonal verlaufenden Linien, der wegen der Höhenbegrenzung in der Region in zwei Abschnitte aufgeteilt wurde, beherbergt die Wohnung eines Ehepaares und ihres Kindes. Beton und Glas werden hier mit Marmor und Aluminium kombiniert. Die typischen Eigenschaften dieser Materialien verleihen dem Gebäude gewöhnlich einen eher soliden und sogar schwerfälligen Charakter. Hier jedoch wurde ein vollkommen gegenteiliger Effekt erreicht. In allen Räumen kommt auf angenehme Weise eine Leichtigkeit zum Ausdruck, die zusammen mit der optimalen Nutzung des Lichtes eine interessante räumliche Sequenz ergibt, die auf dem Kontrast zwischen Licht und Schatten basiert.

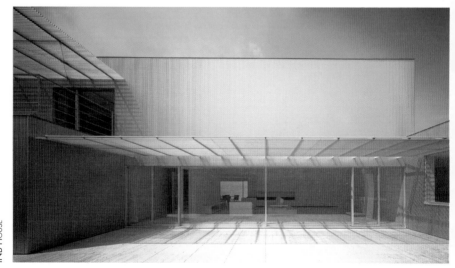

INB HOUSE

A terrace viewpoint has been projected above the dining-room (roof level). A concrete wall protects and defines the perimeter with benches while a pergola projects an attractive light over the area.

Une terrasse-belvédère se projette au-dessus du salon-salle à manger (niveau couvert). Un mur de béton protège et délimite son périmètre au moyen de bancs, et la pergola donne un bel éclairage.

Über dem Wohn- und Esszimmer befindet sich eine Aussichtsterrasse (Dachgeschoss), die durch eine Betonmauer mit eingefaßten Bänken geschützt und nach außen abgegrenzt wird. Durch die Pergola fällt ein angenehmes Licht auf die Terrasse.

INB HOUSE

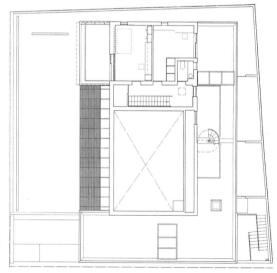

On account of the height restrictions in the area, the house has been organized into two parts. The common spaces of the house and the master bedroom have been laid out on the first floor, while two more bedrooms can be found on the second floor.

A cause des restrictions de hauteur dans la zone, la maison est divisée en deux parties : en bas, les espaces communs de la maison, et deux chambres supplémentaires au premier.

Aufgrund der Höhenbegrenzung in der Region wurde das Haus in zwei Baukörper eingeteilt. Auf der ersten Etage befinden sich gemeinsame Räumlichkeiten des Hauses sowie das Hauptzimmer, während auf die zweite Etage aus zwei weiteren Zimmern besteht.

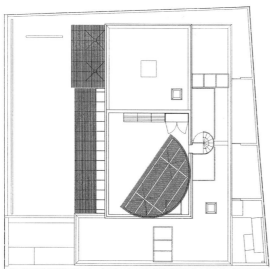

The spatial sequence unfolds itself fluidly, the definition of the different parts of the house is established with a minimum of elements in order to permit a flexible use of the space.

La séquence spatiale fluide et la définition des différents éléments de la maison restent minimes afin de permettre une utilisation flexible de l'espace.

Die räumliche Sequenz geht fließend ineinander über und die Anordnung der Räume des Hauses wird mit einem Minimum an Elementen gestaltet, um eine flexible Raumnutzung zu ermöglichen.

INB House

KERN HOUSE

B & E BAUMSCHLAGER-EBERLE

Lochau, Österreich. 1995 / 1996

One of the client's requirements for the placement of this dwelling on the plot, was that it should interfere as little as possible in the views towards the lake. The project revolves mainly around two simple concepts which endow the house with great beauty. On the one hand, the formal proposal is based on a double "skin" which, in addition to providing protection from the weather, allows for a certain transparency both from the interior of the building and towards it. This double skin also benefited the constructive process: while the prefabricated glass casing was built in one week, the wooden elements were constructed on site. On the other hand, the spatial proposal based on fluidity allowed for the elimination of the boundaries between the different areas.

Une des exigences du client quant à l'emplacement de cette maison était qu'il interfère le moins possible avec les vues sur le lac. Le projet repose principalement sur deux concepts simples qui donnent beaucoup de charme à la maison. D'un côté, la proposition formelle est basée sur une double enveloppe extérieure, qui en plus de protéger des intempéries, crée des transparences aussi bien depuis le bâtiment que vers celui-ci. Cette double protection a également été utilisée au bénéfice du processus constructif : alors qu'il a fallu une semaine pour construire la structure de verre préfabriquée, les éléments de bois ont été montés sur place. D'un autre côté, la proposition spatiale, basée sur la fluidité, permet de faire disparaître les limites entre les différentes fonctions de la maison.

Eine der Anforderungen des Auftraggebers für die Anordnung dieses Wohnhauses auf dem Grundstück war, dass die Aussichten auf den See so gering wie möglich beeinflusst werden sollten. Das Projekt basiert hauptsächlich auf zwei einfachen Konzepten, durch die dem Haus ein stilvoller Charme verliehen wird. Auf der einen Seite basiert die formelle Gestaltung auf einer doppelten Begrenzung, durch die das Gebäude von klimatischen Einflüssen geschützt wird und eine Transparenz sowohl von innen nach außen als auch umgekehrt wurde. Die doppelte Begrenzung wurde auch bei der Errichtung zum Vorteil. Während der Baukörper aus Glas in einer Woche vorgefertigt wurde, wurden die Elemente aus Holz vor Ort errichtet. Auf der anderen Seite basiert die räumliche Gestaltung auf fließenden Übergängen, durch die die Abgrenzungen zwischen den verschiedenen Räumen verschwimmen.

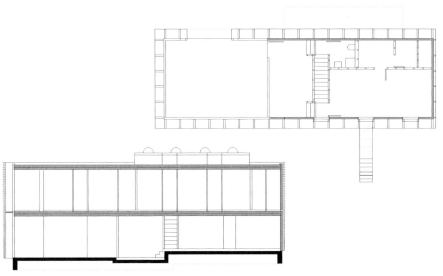

KERN HOUSE

Spatial fluidity also permits versatility in the use of the spaces, for example in the case of the entrance level where different activities can be carried out indiscriminately.

La fluidité spatiale permet des espaces variés, comme par exemple le niveau d'accès qui peut réunir différentes activités.

Durch die fließenden Übergänge zwischen den Räumen wird den Bereichen Flexibilität verliehen, wie zum Beispiel der Eingangsbereich, der auf ganz verschiedene Arten genutzt werden kann.

KERN HOUSE

Wohnhaus in Köln-Müngersdorf

Döring, Dahmen, Joeressen Architekten

Köln-Müngersdorf, Deutschland. 1997

In this project –part of a group of dwellings from the 1930's– the height of the house and its development over 4 floors suggested structuring the areas around a hollow vertical space. Thus a central nucleus, which also holds a staircase, is used as the organizational basis for the entire house. The treatment of the roof of this "empty chimney" permits the introduction of light from overhead, thus converting the chimney into the light transmitter for the dwelling. Formally this central void is reflected in the intersection of the zinc roof where it is divided into two areas forming equilateral triangles.

Dans ce projet, qui fait partie d'un lotissement datant des années 30, la hauteur de la maison et sa répartition sur quatre étages suggère l'agencement des pièces de la maison autour d'un vide aux proportions verticales. De cette manière, le noyau central, qui renferme un escalier, sert de base d'organisation à toute la maison. Le travail du toit qui recouvre cette "cheminée vide" permet la projection zénithale de la lumière et sa diffusion dans toute la maison. Ce vide central est reflété à travers l'intersection avec le toit de zinc, qu'il sépare en deux triangles équilatéraux.

In diesem Projekt, das Bestandteil eines Komplexes der 30er Jahre bildet, wird durch die Höhe des Hauses und seine Gliederung in vier Etagen die räumliche Anordnung um einen leeren Bereich mit vertikalen Proportionen bestimmt. Somit wird ein zentraler Kern, in dem sich auch eine Treppe befindet, als Element zur Gliederung des gesamten Hauses genutzt. Durch die Gestaltung des Daches dieses "leeren Kamins" kann das Licht senkrecht einfallen, wodurch wiederum dieser zentrale Abschnitt zum Element wird, durch das das Haus beleuchtet wird. In formeller Hinsicht wird das Zinkdach durch diesen Leerraum durchbrochen und in zwei Abschnitte eingeteilt, die zwei gleichseitige Dreiecke bilden.

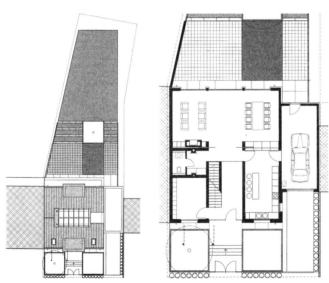

WOHNHAUS IN KÖLN-MUNGERSDORF

Due to the height of this house, a space with a vertical orientation is proposed, which forms the basis for the spatial distribution of the program.

Dû à la hauteur du bâtiment, on propose le développement vertical de l'espace, qui a pour fonction la distribution spatiale du projet.

Aufgrund der Höhe dieses Hauses wird ein vertikal angeordneter Bereich geplant, auf dem die räumliche Anordnung des Programmes basiert.

HOUSE KOSKETUS "TOUCH"

HEIKKINEN-KOMONEN ARCHITECTS, ANTTI KÖNÖNEN

Tuusula, Finland. 1998-2000

Planning a project with a full understanding of the essence of the problem and resolving this problem without tying oneself down to any particular convention appears to be one of the main propositions of these Finnish architects. This is reflected in their attractive project for a prefabricated industrial wooden house whose prototype was built in the Tuusula Exhibition in the year 2000. A volume with clear, simple lines fills the space completely, defining the perimeter in this manner. Nonetheless, in a subsequent sculpting and casting job, exterior spaces were created which are contained within the house. These external areas permit a wide spatial variety in the interior while at the same time transmitting an attractive natural lighting.

Réaliser un projet en comprenant le fond du problème et sans être lié à aucune convention semble être l'un des principaux fondements de ces architectes finlandais, qui se reflète dans ce séduisant projet : une maison industrielle préfabriquée en bois, dont le prototype fut construit lors de l'Exposition de Tuusula 2000. Un bâtiment aux lignes simples et nettes occupe tout l'espace et définit par là même le périmètre à utiliser. Néanmoins, à travers un travail ultérieur de sculptage et de moulage, des espaces extérieurs se créent depuis la maison, ce qui offre une grande diversité spatiale intérieure tout en communiquant une agréable lumière naturelle.

Beim Gestalten von Entwürfen sollte man das Problem in seiner Essenz begreifen und eine Lösung finden, ohne an jegliche Konventionen gebunden zu sein. Dies ist wohl eines der Hauptanliegen dieser finnischen Architekten und spiegelt sich in diesem ansprechenden Projekt wider, einem vorgefertigten Industriehaus aus Holz, dessen Prototyp auf der Wohnungsmesse in Tuusula im Jahr 2000 gebaut wurde. Ein Baukörper einfacher und klarer Linien füllt gänzlich den Raum und bestimmt somit den geplanten Umfang. Durch späteres Meißeln und Entleeren entstehen jedoch äußere Räume, die durch das Haus zusammengehalten werden und dem Innenraum ein hohes Maß an räumlicher Vielfalt und gleichzeitig eine angenehme natürliche Beleuchtung verleihen.

234

This prefabricated house was originally designed for a family of 4, as it could reach a total of 140 m². of constructed area. The versatility of its structure permits the house to be adapted to different settings.

Ce logement préfabriqué a été initialement conçu pour une famille de quatre personnes, et peut atteindre jusqu'à 140 m² habitables. Grâce à sa pluralité, cette maison peut s'adapter à différents emplacements.

Dieses vorgefertigte Haus wurde ursprünglich für eine vierköpfige Familie entworfen und hat eine Oberfläche von 140 m². Durch die Flexibilität seines Baukörpers kann das Haus an verschiedene Standorte angepasst werden.

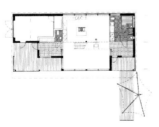

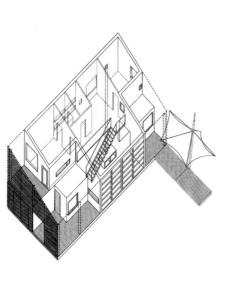

CASA LA CRUZ

LEGORRETA + LEGORRETA

Los Tamarindos, México. 2000

The Tamarindo region, on the Pacific coast of Mexico, offers two physical and visual possibilities: one towards the sea and the other, the forest. The design proposed here concerns two dwellings, La Cruz and Las Terrazas Houses, which were charged with the mission of demonstrating the charms of living "within the forest". The first house, situated atop a hillside, was designed in the shape of a cross. The different orientations suggested by this organizational style make it possible to avoid focusing on any one single aspect, while at the same time facilitating other aspects of the design: the exploitation of all the different perspectives over the area, cross ventilation and an optimum adaptation to the terrain.

La zone du Tamarindo, sur la côte pacifique mexicaine, offre deux possibilités physiques et visuelles vers la mer ou vers la forêt. Le projet en question comporte deux maisons, Casa La Cruz et Las Terrazas, qui témoignent du charme de la vie "dans la forêt". Cette première maison, située en haut d'une colline, est conçue avec une planimétrie cruciforme. Les différentes orientations suggérées par ce type d'organisation évitent de s'engager dans une seule direction car elles favorisent d'autres aspects propres à la conception : l'exploitation de toutes les perspectives sur le lieu, l'aération croisée, et une excellente adaptation au terrain.

Das Meer auf der einen und der Regenwald auf der anderen Seite bilden sowohl optische als auch physische Vorzüge in doppelter Hinsicht in der Region des Tamarindo an der Pazifikküste Mexikos. Die Planung für dieses Gebiet besteht aus zwei Projekten, den Häusern Casa La Cruz und Las Terrazas, in denen der Vorteil geboten werden soll, "im Regenwald" zu leben. Das erste auf einem Hügel errichtete Haus wurde mit einer kreuzförmigen Planimetrie entworfen. Durch die somit entstehenden unterschiedlichen Ausrichtungen des Gebäudes muss sich nicht nur mit einer Frontseite abgefunden werden. Gleichzeitig werden durch den kreuzförmigen Entwurf auch andere Vorzüge geboten, wie die Nutzung aller Perspektiven über den Standort, die Belüftung und eine optimale Anpassung an das Gelände.

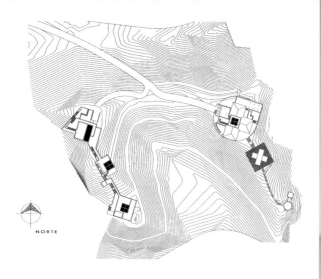

NORTE

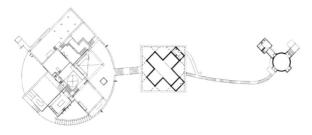

The swimming pool is situated on a lower hillside. Its shape, as in the case of the house, is that of a cross. The entire pool is contained within a wooden platform which slips into the forest.

Sur une colline un peu plus bas se trouve la piscine, qui, de même que la maison, forme une croix. Elle repose entièrement sur une plate-forme en bois qui rejoint la forêt.

Auf einem etwas niedrigeren Hügel befindet sich der Swimmingpool. Seine Form ist kreuzförmig, genau wie das Haus. Er wird komplett in eine hölzerne Plattform eingeschlossen, die zum Regenwald hin ausgerichtet ist.

With a simple organizational scheme in the floor plan it was possible to exploit the virtues of the location to the utmost. Hence, in addition to optimising the design process, the effects on the surroundings were kept to a minimum.

Grâce à un plan d'organisation simple, on arrive à exploiter au maximum les qualités du site. Ainsi, on peut tirer profit du concept tout en respectant les conditions environnantes.

Durch die einfache Anordnung der Innenräume können die Vorzüge des Standortes maximal ausgeschöpft werden. Somit wird nicht nur der Prozess des Entwurfes optimiert, sondern auch in die Beschaffenheit des Standortes so gering wie möglich eingegriffen.

CASA LA CRUZ

CASA LAS TERRAZAS

LEGORRETA + LEGORRETA

Los Tamarindos, México. 2001

This is the second house built in the development proposed for the Tamarindo region. Its location towards the interior obliges it to relate more directly with the forest rather than the sea, although it preserves its views over the latter. The proposal in this case is for a composition of a linear nature divided into three pavilions connected by stairways. Each of the rooftops of these pavilions is used as a terrace or swimming pool, which generates an attractive exterior spatial sequence. The "free" positioning of the pavilions allows them to adapt themselves easily to the terrain.

Cette maison est la deuxième construite au sein du projet développé dans la région du Tamarindo. Sa position, vers l'intérieur, la rattache plus directement à la forêt qu'à la mer, bien qu'elle conserve un angle de vision sur cette dernière. Le projet est une composition au caractère linéaire, divisée en trois pavillons reliés par un parcours d'escaliers. Chacun des toits de ces pavillons fait office de terrasse avec piscine, ce qui crée un séduisant schéma spatial extérieur. L'emplacement "libre" des pavillons permet une adaptation facile au terrain.

Dies ist das zweite Haus, das im Rahmen der geplanten Entwicklung in der Region von Tamarindo errichtet wurde. Da sich sein Standort weiter im Landesinneren befindet, verbindet man es direkter mit der Gegend des Regenwaldes als mit dem Meer, das von dort aus trotzdem gesehen werden kann. In der Planung dieses Projektes ist ein linearer Stil vorrangig. Es ist in drei Pavillons eingeteilt, die wiederum durch einen Treppengang miteinander verbunden sind. Jede einzelne Überdachung dieser Pavillons wird als Terrasse oder Swimmingpool genutzt, wodurch eine interessante räumliche Sequenz der Außenbereiche entsteht. Der "freie" Standort der Pavillons erleichtert die Anpassung an das Gelände.

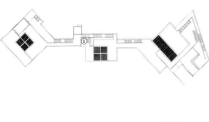

The proposal of terraces and swimming pools on the rooftops of the pavilions enables the surroundings to be enjoyed from the most privileged areas while at the same time creating an attractive exterior spatial sequence.

Le concept de terrasses et piscines sur les toits des pavillons permet de profiter du site depuis les zones les plus privilégiées, et constitue une séquence spatiale extérieure attrayante.

Die Planung der Terrassen und Swimmingpools auf den Decken der Pavillons ermöglichen einen Genuss des Standortes von den einzigartigen Bereichen aus, und zur gleichen Zeit wird eine attraktive räumliche Sequenz der Außenbereiche geschaffen.

The respect for the conditions in the region demonstrated in the proposals for Las Terrazas and La Cruz Houses establishes a precedent for future construction in the Tamarindo region.

Le respect des conditions environnantes fait des projets Casa de Las Terrazas et Casa de la Cruz les précurseurs de futures constructions dans la zone du Tamarindo.

Der Respekt der Beschaffenheit der Gegend gegenüber in der Planung der Häuser Casa de Las Terrazas und Casa de la Cruz setzt einen Präzedenzfall für zukünftige Bauprojekte in der Region von Tamarindo.

CASA EN LA PUNTA

ALFONSO LÓPEZ BAZ, JAVIER CALLEJA

México DF, México. 1998

The residential area where this project was built is composed of houses representing a variety of different styles. As a result the new house was closed off from the exterior in order to avoid contributing to the stylistic chaos which reigns in the neighbourhood. This condition made it possible to propose an enclosed volume resting upon an elevated surface. Formal variety was achieved using stone walls and small, translucent pieces which enhance the impenetrable character of the dwelling. In its spatial proposal, an inner courtyard was the starting point for the organization of the program which made it possible to preserve the privacy necessary to a residence as well as controlling the visibility of the building from the exterior.

Le quartier résidentiel dans lequel se trouve ce projet est constitué de maisons aux styles différents. Ainsi, cette nouvelle construction se ferme sur l'extérieur afin d'éviter d'ajouter au chaos stylistique de la zone. Cette caractéristique permet de proposer une volumétrie fermée qui s'appuie sur une superficie élevée. On obtient une variété des formes grâce aux plans de pierre et aux petites pièces translucides qui conservent intacte la nature hermétique de l'ensemble. Le projet s'organise à partir d'un patio intérieur qui permet de préserver l'intimité de la maison et de contrôler les différents points de vue sur cette dernière.

Das Wohngebiet, in dem dieses Projekt errichtet wird, besteht aus Häusern verschiedener Baustile. Aus diesem Grund wird das neue Wohnhaus nach außen hin geschlossen, um das stilistische Chaos der Umgebung nicht noch zusätzlich zu erhöhen. Durch diese Bedingungen kann eine geschlossene Volumetrie geschaffen werden, die sich auf eine angehobene Oberfläche stützt. Die formelle Vielfalt wird durch Flächen aus Stein und kleine transparente Elemente erreicht, wodurch dem Gesamtwerk ein hermetischer Eindruck verliehen wird. Was die räumliche Anordnung betrifft, wird das Programm ausgehend von einem Innenhof organisiert, durch den die nötige Privatsphäre erhalten und gleichzeitig die Sicht auf das Wohnhaus gewährleistet wird.

Different geometric proposals, walls with aluminium shades and vaulted roofs create singular openings for the passage of light.

Les solutions géométriques variées, les persiennes en aluminium et les toitures voûtées permettent d'intéressantes projections de lumière dans la maison.

Durch die verschiedenen geometrischen Anordnungen, die schützenden Flächen aus Aluminium und die schrägen Dächer entstehen interessante Lichteffekte.

CASA EN LA PUNTA

261

VILLA LE GOFF

RUDY RICCIOTTI ARCHITECTE

Marseille, France. 2000

One of the characteristics common to many of the works of this engineer/architect is his respect for the natural surroundings. This is demonstrated by projects such as Villa Lyprendi (1997-1998) or Villa Marmonier (1999), where the architecture itself vanishes into the surrounding countryside. In this residence, situated on a wooded lot with a steep slope descending towards the sea, respect for the location is also the motive for the proposal. Thus, in order to affect the natural environment as little as possible, the house was placed on the upper end of the lot while the living-room and terraces are literally projected over the treetops.

Une des caractéristiques communes à certaines des oeuvres de cet ingénieur/architecte est son respect de l'environnement, ce que démontrent des projets tels que la Villa Lyprendi (1997-1998) ou la Villa Marmonier (1999), où l'architecture elle-même se fond dans le paysage. C'est là aussi le respect de la nature environnante qui est à la base de cette habitation, située dans un terrain boisé avec une forte pente qui descend vers la mer. Afin d'affecter le moins possible le paysage, la maison occupe le haut du terrain ; le salon et les terrasses se projettent littéralement sur la cime des arbres.

Eine der Gemeinsamkeiten einiger Werke des Ingenieurs und Architekten kommen durch seinen Respekt der natürlichen Umgebung gegenüber zum Ausdruck. Dies spiegelt sich beispielsweise in den Projekten Villa Lyprendi (1997-1998) und Villa Marmonier (1999) wider, wo die Architektur selbst in der Natur verschwindet. In diesem Wohnhaus, das sich auf einem bewaldeten Grundstück mit einem starken Gefälle zum Meer befindet, wird die Planung ebenfalls durch den Respekt des Standortes gegenüber beeinflusst. Um die natürliche Umgebung so gering wie möglich zu beeinflussen, wurde das Haus auf dem oberen Abschnitt des Grundstücks errichtet, wodurch das Wohnzimmer und die Terrassen sich geradezu über den Baumkronen befinden.

VILLA LE GOFF

The external protection of the glazed walls is accomplished by a large curtain woven of the same material used by the French Navy as camouflage, which projects an attractive light into the interior.

La protection extérieure des surfaces vitrées est assurée au moyen d'un grand rideau conçu à partir du même matériel que celui que l'armée française utilisait comme camouflage, et qui projette une agréable lumière dans la maison.

Die verglasten Flächen werden nach außen hin durch einen großen Vorhang geschützt. Dieser besteht aus demselben Material, das von der französischen Armee als Tarnung verwendet wird, und lässt ein angenehmes Licht in den Innenraum scheinen.

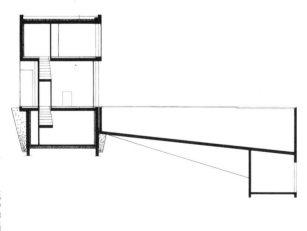

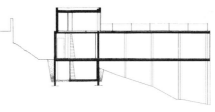

The main block of the dwelling is placed on the upper end of the L-shaped plot, oriented entirely towards the terrace where a pool with views over the sea has been installed.

Le bloc principal de la villa se situe sur la partie supérieure du terrain, avec une planimétrie en L orientée vers la terrasse, qui comprend une piscine avec vue sur la mer.

Der Hauptblock des Wohnhauses befindet sich auf dem oberen Abschnitt des Grundstückes. Die Planimetrie ist L-förmig und zur Terrasse hin ausgerichtet, wo ein Swimmingpool mit Meerblick entsteht.

VILLA LE GOFF

LEVIS HOUSE

UDA; DAVIDE VOLPE

Vandorno, Italia. 1998

This project consists of an addition to a typical rural residence. The relationship between the new rooms and the surrounding area is of vital importance for its planning. Thus, the arrangement of the spaces on the floor plan is developed as a sieve filtering the pathway from the original house to the surrounding landscape through the different areas of the home. This idea is also reflected in the treatment of the volume, to which a group of wooden ribs which reveal but a hint of the interior volume is attached. In this treatment, even the light itself plays an important role, transforming the pathway from the interior to the exterior into an intriguing spatial sequence of uses and lights.

Ce projet consiste à agrandir une maison rurale traditionnelle. La relation entre la nouvelle structure et le lieu qui l'entoure est d'une importance vitale pour sa mise en œuvre. Les étages s'organisent et se développent comme s'ils constituaient un tamis filtrant le parcours depuis l'ancienne maison jusqu'au paysage alentour, à travers les différentes pièces. La même idée est reflétée dans la conception du volume, au-dessus duquel vient s'ajouter un groupe de lattes de bois, qui laissent à peine deviner le volume intérieur. Grâce à cette approche, la lumière joue un rôle important, car elle transforme le parcours de l'intérieur à l'extérieur de la maison en un espace fonctionnel et lumineux.

Dieses Projekt besteht aus einer Erweiterung eines typischen Landhauses. Der Bezug des Anbaus zu seiner Umgebung ist für die Planung von entscheidender Bedeutung. Dementsprechend wurden die Innenräume so angeordnet, als würden sie als Übergang zwischen dem ursprünglichen Haus und der Umgebung dienen. Dies wird auch in der Planung des Baukörpers deutlich, vor dem sich Rippen aus Holz befinden, die dem äußeren Betrachter nur eine Vermutung über die Struktur des Baukörpers gewähren. Auf diese Weise spielt das Licht eine wichtige Rolle, durch das von innen nach außen eine stilvolle räumliche Sequenz geschaffen wird.

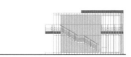

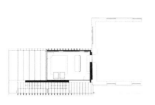

The project was carried out by the team of UdA, founded in 1992 by Walter Camagna, Maximiliano Camoletto and Andrea Marcante.

Ce projet a été réalisé par l'équipe UdA, fondée en 1992 par Walter Camagna, Maximiliano Camoletto et Andrea Marcante.

Das Projekt wurde vom 1992 durch Walter Camagna, Maximiliano Camoletto und Andrea Marcante gegründeten Team UdA durchgeführt.

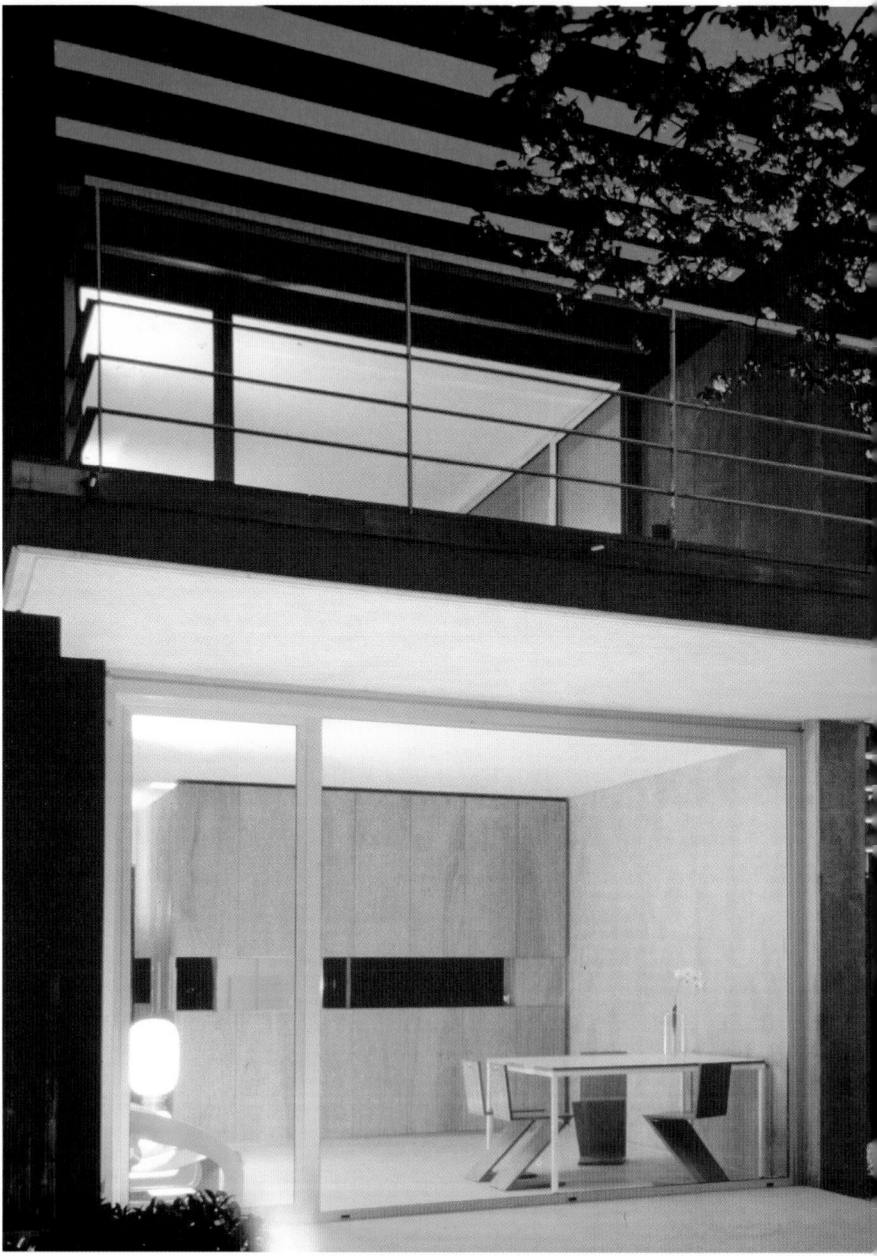

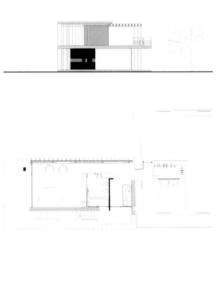

Due to the conditions in the area which was cultivated as a vegetable garden and oriented towards the Alps, the architectural proposal strives to reflect the importance of the relationship between the new elements and the location.

Dû aux caractéristiques du terrain, cultivé à la manière d'un jardin potager et s'orientant vers les Alpes, la proposition architecturale cherche à refléter l'importance des relations entre le nouvel élément et le lieu où il se trouve.

Aufgrund der Beschaffenheit des Standortes, der als Gemüsegarten genutzt wird und in Richtung Alpen ausgerichtet ist, soll durch die architektonische Planung die Bedeutung der Beziehungen des neuen Elements zur Umgebung widergespiegelt werden.

LEVIS HOUSE

VILLA LYPRENDI

RUDY RICCIOTTI ARCHITECTE

Toulon, France. 1997-1998

The locality where this residence was constructed presents a number of projects built according to a pronounced regionalist tradition in the surrounding architecture. This situation has reinforced the conceptual posture of the project since the architect, by means of a radical proposal, has succeeded in making even the architecture itself vanish in favour of the environment, unlike the usual procedure in the traditional homes. As a result the architectural definition of this house is accomplished with few elements: a glass wall and a partially overhanging platform. This large glazed wall 35 m. in length and 2,60 m. high is the only façade on the house, whose volume is practically non-existent.

On trouve autour de l'emplacement de cette villa un lotissement construit dans une grande tradition architecturale régionaliste. Cette condition a promu la position conceptuelle de ce projet : l'architecte, par une composition radicale, fait disparaître la structure elle-même en faveur du milieu environnant, contrairement à ce qui se fait dans les maisons traditionnelles. En conséquence, la définition architecturale de cette villa est obtenue avec peu d'éléments : une surface vitrée et une plate-forme partiellement en porte-à-faux. Ce grand vitrage de 35 m de long sur 2,60 m de haut constitue l'unique façade de la maison, dont le volume est pratiquement inexistant.

Dieses Wohnhaus befindet sich in einer Gegend, in der sich die umliegenden Projekte architektonisch durch eine markante regionale Tradition auszeichnen. Diese kompromißlose Situation hat den konzeptuellen Standpunkt des Architekten bei der Entwicklung des Projektes entscheidend beeinflusst. Der Umgebung zuliebe lässt er die Architektur verschwinden, ganz im Gegensatz zu den traditionellen Häusern. Aus diesem Grund wird die Architektur dieses Hauses mit wenigen Elementen, einer Glasfläche und einer teilweise ausgekragten Plattform, entwickelt. Die große verglaste Fläche mit einer Breite von 35 m und einer Höhe von 2,60 m ist die einzige Fassade des Hauses, dessen Baukörper praktisch nicht existiert.

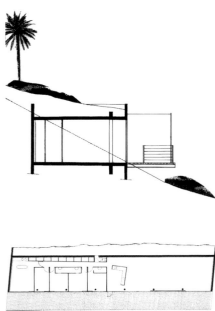

The extreme natural conditions in the area, with a steep 45° slope, favoured the proposal of one of the main defining elements in the project: a platform sustained partly in cantilever which runs along the length of the façade.

Les conditions naturelles extrêmes, avec une forte pente de 45°, favorisent l'élaboration d'un des éléments clés du projet : une plate-forme partiellement en porte-à-faux qui suit la façade sur toute sa longueur.

Durch die extremen natürlichen Bedingungen der Umgebung mit einer Grundstücksneigung von 45° wird die Planung eines der Hauptelemente bestärkt, durch die das Projekt besticht, eine teilweise ausgekragte Plattform, die sich über die Gesamtlänge der Fassade ausdehnt.

VILLA LYPRENDI

CASA MAHNS

LUIS IZQUIERDO, ANTONIA LEHMANN

Vitacura, Chile. 1998-1999

Although the professional experience of these Chilean architects includes several single-family dwellings, they have no preconceived model. Each project is a new challenge where the program, the location and the construction work are the factors which provide the foundation for the project. For this house, located on the side of Manquehue Hill, a singular "dock-house" which soars over the slope is proposed. Its design over several floors allows these floors to become natural extensions of the different levels existing on the terrain, thus creating an intriguing spatial sequence which is developed across the slope.

En dépit des nombreux logements individuels qui constituent l'expérience professionnelle de ces architectes chiliens, il n'existe pas pour eux de modèle préconçu. Chaque œuvre est un nouveau défi où le plan, le site et la construction ont pour fonction de donner les caractéristiques linéaires du projet. Dans cette habitation, située sur le flanc de la colline Manquehue, s'érige une intéressante "maison à ressorts" qui survole la pente. Les différents étages forment les extensions naturelles des niveaux existants du terrain, ce qui crée une séquence spatiale suggestive qui progresse le long de la pente.

Obgleich diese chilenischen Architekten in ihrer beruflichen Laufbahn eine große Anzahl von Einfamilienhäusern entwarfen, gibt es für sie kein Standardmodell. Jedes Haus ist eine neue Herausforderung, und die Richtlinien für jedes Projekt wird durch die individuelle Planung, den Standort und die Bauweise bestimmt. Dieses Haus, das sich am Abhang der Anhöhe Manquehue befindet, gleicht einer Rampe, die förmlich über dem Abhang schwebt. Es ist in verschiedene Etagen eingeteilt, die wie natürliche Erweiterungen der unterschiedlichen Höhen des Geländes wirken. Durch das Einbinden des Hauses in den Abhang wird eine attraktive räumliche Sequenz geschaffen.

As a result of the development over different levels the proposal of a vertical connection is of vital importance within the home. Thus a great connecting space joins the different levels using stairways and bridges.

Pour le développement de ce logement à plusieurs niveaux, le concept de rattachement vertical est d'une importance vitale. Ainsi, un grand espace sert d'élément de connexion entre les différents niveaux à travers des escaliers et des ponts.

Durch die Einteilung des Projektes in verschiedene Etagen ist die Planung des vertikalen Bezugs im Innenraum von großer Bedeutung. Somit werden die Etagen in einem großräumigen Bereich durch Treppen und Brücken miteinander verbunden.

CASA MAHNS

VILLA MARIA

SETH STEIN ARCHITECTS

Osterskorvon, Finland. 2000

This house is situated on a small island in the Finnish Archipelago, 80 km. from the capital. The almost uninhabited island provides no infrastructures, which obliged the approach to the project to be based upon constructive and energetic logic. Thus these two criteria became decisive while developing the proposal. On the one hand the possibility of building prefabricated pieces off the island was studied, in order to assemble them later *in situ*. On the other hand, taking advantage of the solar and wind power in the area in order to generate energy in the house was proposed. Formally, a delicate glass and wood building glides subtly into the local vegetation.

Cette maison se trouve dans une petite île de l'archipel finlandais, à 80 Km de la capitale. L'île, qui compte très peu d'habitants, ne bénéficie pas d'infrastructures, ce qui oblige à aborder le projet avec une logique constructive et énergétique, deux aspects décisifs au bon déroulement de la construction. D'un côté, on étudie la possibilité de construire des pièces préfabriquées en dehors de l'île pour ensuite les assembler sur place. D'un autre côté, on propose d'exploiter l'énergie solaire et éolienne de la zone pour alimenter la maison. La subtilité des formes de cette délicate construction de verre et de bois se fond dans la végétation.

Dieses Haus steht auf einer kleinen Insel des finnischen Archipels, 80 km von der Hauptstadt entfernt. Die fast unbewohnte Insel verfügt über keine Infrastruktur, wodurch die Bauweise und Nutzung der Energie des Projektes an diese Lage angepasst werden musste. Zwei Punkte sind also bei der Entwicklung der Planung von entscheidender Bedeutung. Auf der einen Seite werden die Möglichkeiten untersucht, die Bestandteile des Hauses außerhalb der Insel anzufertigen, um die vorgefertigten Teile später vor Ort zusammenzufügen. Auf der anderen Seite wird bei geplant, die Sonnen- und Windenergie des Standorts für das Haus zu nutzen. In formeller Hinsicht wird eine zerbrechliche Baustruktur aus Glas und Holz auf diskrete Weise in die Pflanzenwelt der Umgebung eingegliedert.

The structure of the house is based on the standard measurements for photovoltaic panels. A delicate curved roof contains the 12 panels necessary to the functioning of the residence.

La structure de la villa suit les mesures standards des panneaux photovoltaïques. Un élégant toit incurvé contient les douze panneaux nécessaires au fonctionnement de l'habitat.

Die Struktur des Hauses basiert auf den Standardmaßen der Sonnenkollektoren. Auf einem stilvollen gekrümmten Dach sind zwölf Platten angeordnet, die zur Energieversorgung des Haushaltes notwendig sind.

VILLA MARIA

The client wished to place the residence on the highest point of the island in order to enjoy a 360° panorama. This was possible thanks to the commitment to the development of a plan whereby the silhouette of the house would be contained within that of the trees.

Le client souhaitait une habitation sur le point le plus haut de l'île afin de jouir d'une vue de 360°. Ceci a été rendu possible grâce au développement d'une structure où la silhouette de la maison épouse celle des arbres.

Nach den Wünschen des Auftraggebers sollte das Wohnhaus den höchsten Punkt der Insel bilden, um einen Ausblick rund um die Insel genießen zu können. Dies wurde durch die Entwicklung eines Schemas ermöglicht, in dem die Kontur des Hauses über die der Bäume herausragt.

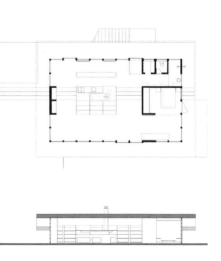

VILLA MARIA

Villa Marmonier

Rudy Ricciotti Architecte

La Garde, France. 1999

This project consisted of the expansion and rehabilitation of a 1930's residence. The expansion was carried out with a simple rectangular volume combining concrete, wood and glass. As in the case of Villa Lyprendi (1997-1998), the structure tends to vanish into the surroundings, producing a remarkable design of vertical and horizontal planes. In this manner, the glazed wall of the façade appears to vanish beneath the roof. The platform of the terrace, which blends in with the interior and the swimming pool to form a unit, is presented as a third, horizontal element.

Ce projet consiste à agrandir et à réhabiliter une maison construite dans les années 30. L'agrandissement s'effectue au moyen d'un simple volume rectangulaire où se combinent béton, bois et verre. Comme pour la Villa Lyprendi (1997-1998), la volumétrie a tendance à disparaître en faveur de l'environnement, ce qui ouvre la voie à un intéressant travail de plans verticaux et horizontaux. Ainsi, la surface vitrée de la façade s'efface visuellement sous le toit. La plate-forme de la terrasse constitue le troisième élément – horizontal cette fois – de cette maison ; elle forme un tout avec l'intérieur et la piscine.

Im Rahmen dieses Projektes wird ein Wohnhaus der 30er Jahre ausgebaut und saniert. Der Anbau besteht aus einem einfachen rechteckigen Baukörper, bei dessen Bau Beton, Holz und Glas verwendet werden. Wie auch bei der Villa Lyprendi (1997-1998) ist die Volumetrie in der Umgebung kaum wahrnehmbar, wodurch Grund- und Aufriss auf interessante Weise gestaltet werden können. Somit ist die gläserne Fläche der Fassade unter dem Dach nicht zu sehen. Ein drittes in diesem Fall horizontal angeordnetes Element ist die Terrasse, durch deren Plattform der Innenraum mit dem Swimmingpool verbunden wird.

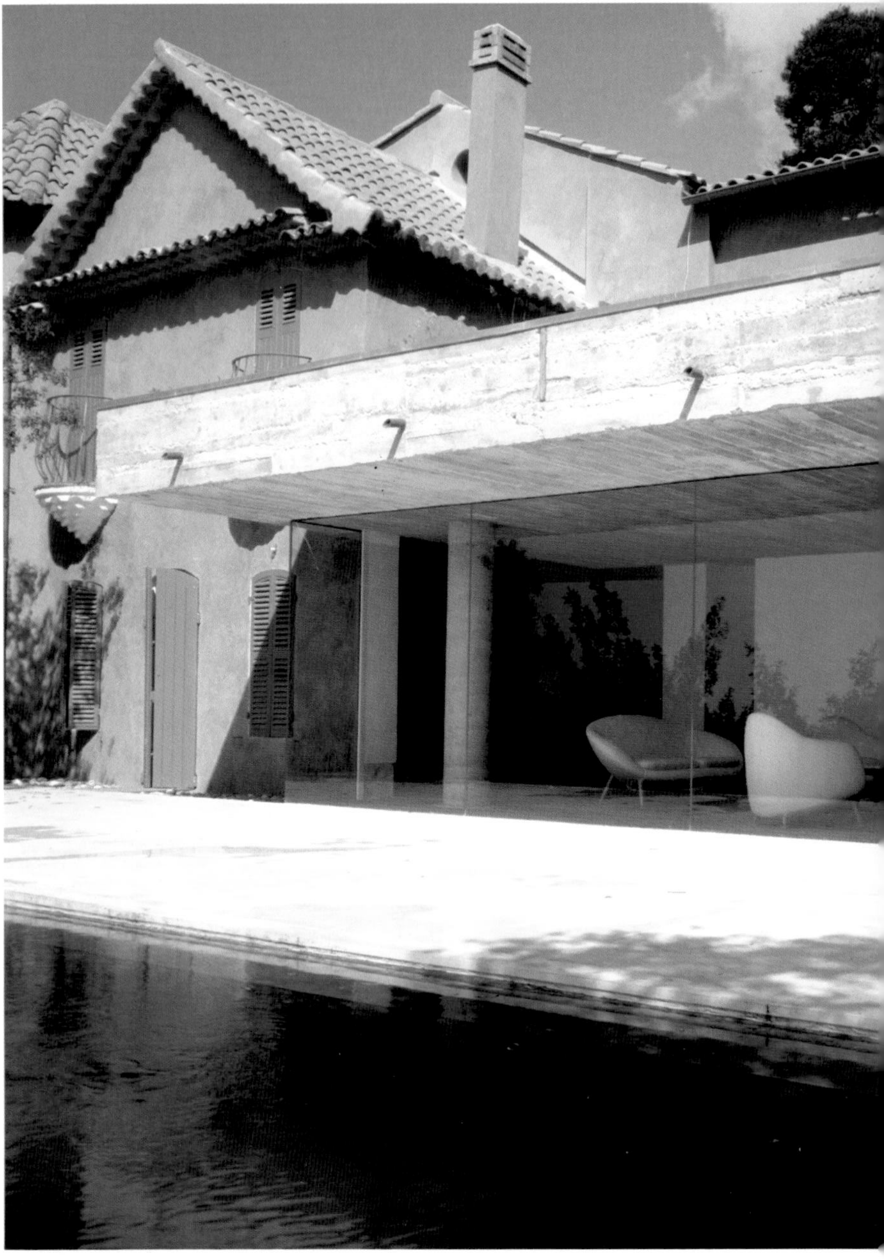

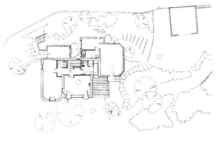

The project encompassed the expansion and restoration of a 1930's villa, with a program which included a terrace, a swimming pool, an addition and interior and exterior rehabilitation, as well as the rehabilitation of a summerhouse near the residence.

Ce projet envisage l'agrandissement et la rénovation d'une villa des années 30, qui comprend la construction d'une terrasse et d'une piscine, une extension, la réhabilitation intérieure et extérieure ainsi que la transformation d'un pavillon proche de la villa.

Die Entwicklung des Projektes sieht eine Erweiterung und Sanierung einer Villa der 30er Jahre vor. Die Planung schließt eine Terrasse, einen Swimmingpool, einen Anbau, die Sanierung der Innen- und Außenräume, sowie den Ausbau eines Pavillons in der Nähe des Wohnhauses ein.

VILLA MARMONIER

A large terrace running down the length of the house forms the horizontal border which contains the addition. This terrace stretches from the interior to the swimming pool passing through a number of changes in its flooring.

Une grande terrasse qui s'étend le long de la maison devient un plan horizontal qui abrite la construction annexe, changeant de carrelage entre l'intérieur et la piscine.

Die große Terrasse, die der Gesamtlänge des Hauses entspricht, ist ein horizontaler Bereich, der den Anbau bildet und gleichzeitig auf stilvolle Weise den Innenraum mit dem Swimmingpool verbindet.

RESIDENCE MEERBUSCH

ARCHITEKT ALEXANDER VOIGT

Meerbusch, Deutschland. 1999

This house is located in a residential area characterized by dwellings built in the 1970's. As in the case of several other residential complexes, the position of this dwelling forced the designer to propose a different treatment for each of the two main façades on the building. This dual condition was kept in mind right from the start of the project. Thus an almost completely closed-in volume offers very little in terms of its views towards the street where it is located. Nevertheless, as one moves away from the front of the house, little by little the house begins to open up until finally it becomes transformed into a large roof with glazed walls. In this manner, as one approaches the rear façade the volume itself disappears, transforming itself into a series of vertical and horizontal planes which define the arrangement of the program.

Cette habitation se situe dans une zone résidentielle caractérisée par des logements des années 70. Comme c'est le cas dans beaucoup d'autres complexes résidentiels, l'emplacement de cette maison a obligé l'auteur à proposer un traitement différent pour chacune des deux devantures principales dont il dispose, double condition présente dès le début du projet. Ainsi, un volume pratiquement fermé offre peu de concessions visuelles vers la rue sur laquelle il donne. Mais plus on s'éloigne de cette façade, plus il s'ouvre pour finalement se transformer en une grande toiture vitrée. De cette manière, la façade arrière et le volume s'effacent pour faire place à des plans verticaux et horizontaux qui délimitent l'organisation de la résidence.

Dieses Wohnhaus befindet sich in einem Wohngebiet, das sich durch Wohnhäuser im Stil der 70er Jahre auszeichnet. Wie auch bei vielen anderen Wohnraumerschließungen wird die Planung des Architekten durch den Standort dieses Gebäudes eingeschränkt. Die zwei Hauptfassaden des Hauses müssen demnach jeweils unterschiedlich entworfen werden, als bei der Planung von Anfang an in Betracht gezogen wird. Dementsprechend werden durch einen fast geschlossenen Baukörper nur wenige Aussichten auf die anliegende Straße geboten. Die hintere Fassade jedoch öffnet sich jedoch dem Außenraum durch große verglaste Flächen. Somit wird durch das Design der hinteren Fassade der eigentliche Baukörper als solcher nicht wahrgenommen, sondern nur die vertikalen und horizontalen Flächen, durch die das Programm angeordnet ist.

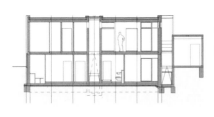

The division of the volume into two parts also determines the arrangement of the spaces of the program. Hence the service areas and kitchen are placed near the street, while the rest areas and common areas are located in the rear.

Le volume se divise en deux pour distribuer les différentes fonctions de la maison. Dans la zone qui donne sur la rue, on trouve salle de bains et cuisine, tandis que l'arrière renferme les chambres et les salles communes.

Durch die Aufteilung des Baukörpers in zwei Abschnitte wird auch die Nutzung des Projektes aufgeteilt. Im Bereich zur Strasse befinden sich Bad und Küche, während im hinteren Bereich die Schlaf- und das Wohnzimmer angeordnet sind.

RESIDENCE MEERBUSCH

PRIVATE ESTATE IN MONTANA

EMILIO AMBASZ & ASSOCIATES

Montana, USA. 1992-1995

Situated in an attractive natural scenic area, this house belongs to an estate which also includes the guard's house, a private art gallery and a small meditation pavilion. The structural handling permits the surrounding nature to flow over the ensemble leaving a large glazed façade as the only visible element. In this manner a new interpretation of the regional tradition is proposed, which consists of covering the rooftops of the cabins with earth. In this singular home even the materials themselves are reinterpreted in order to be used in innovative forms, for example the colonnade of tree trunks and their cornices which catch the light reflections from the surroundings.

Située dans un agréable site naturel, cette maison fait partie d'un ensemble qui abrite également la maison du garde, une galerie d'art privée et un petit pavillon de méditation. Le traitement des volumes permet à la nature de suivre son cours le long de ce complexe, avec comme seul élément visible une grande façade vitrée. De cette manière, l'auteur propose une nouvelle interprétation de la tradition locale qui consiste à recouvrir de terre les toits des cabanes. Dans cette singulière maison, les matériaux acquièrent une nouvelle fonction et s'utilisent de forme innovatrice, comme par exemple l'arcade formée de troncs et la corniche qui se chargent de capturer les reflets lumineux du site.

Dieses Haus wurde in einem wunderschönen Naturpark errichtet und gehört zu einem Gesamtwerk, das auch das Pförtnerhaus, eine private Kunstgalerie und einen kleinen Meditationspavillon beherbergt. Durch die Anordnung der Volumetrie kann die Natur förmlich über das Haus hinweg fließen. Das einzig sichtbare Element ist eine große verglaste Fassade. Diese Planung wurde gemäß der regionalen Tradition gestaltet, die darin besteht, die Dächer der Hütten mit Erde zu bedecken. In diesem einzigartigen Haus werden die Materialien selbst neu interpretiert, um sie auf eine innovative Weise zu nutzen, wie beispielsweise der Säulengang aus Baumstämmen und sein Gesims, in denen die Lichtreflexe des Standortes eingefangen werden sollen.

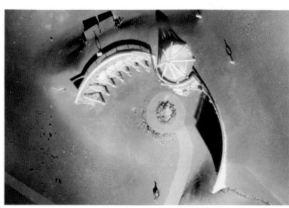

One of the requirements of the owners of the estate was that the project should demonstrate respect for the location, making every attempt to keep the visual impact on the area to a minimum, while at the same time reflecting the family preference for classical styles.

Une des exigences des propriétaires de ce domaine était le respect de l'endroit et le moindre impact visuel possible sur la zone, ainsi que l'élaboration d'un projet reflétant le goût familial pour le style classique.

Eine der Bedingungen der Eigentümer des Gebäudes war, dass das Projekt den Standort respektieren sollte. Daher unternahm man den Versuch, optisch in die Umgebung so gering wie möglich einzugreifen und gleichzeitig dem Geschmack der Familie für den klassischen Stil zu folgen.

Mt. Martha Beach House

BBP Architects

Victoria, Australia. 2001 / 2002

In the cases of beachside residences, the formal and spatial proposals for the projects are directly related to the typology of the settings and their characteristics. This statement is confirmed by this residence located near the city of Melbourne, where the Miesian concept of "less is more" is worked out in detail in order to endow the project with great beauty and simplicity. A group of geometrically pure volumes —some of which fit snugly into the terrain while others are supported by a simple structure— generates a formal composition of solid and empty spaces which produce a compelling play of transparencies and reflections.

Dans les maisons situées sur la plage, le schéma formel et spatial du projet est étroitement lié à la typologie et aux caractéristiques du site. Cette habitation située près de Melbourne vient confirmer cette idée, avec des concepts miesiens où "moins signifie plus", qui donnent naissance à un projet simple et fascinant. Un groupe de volumes géométriquement purs, dont les uns s'imbriquent dans le terrain tandis que d'autres s'appuient sur une structure simple, forment une composition formelle de solides et de vides qui offre un intéressant jeu de transparences et de reflets.

Die formelle und räumliche Planung von Strandhäusern steht in direktem Bezug zur Typologie und der Beschaffenheit des Standortes. Das ist auch bei diesem Wohnhaus in der Nähe der Stadt Melbourne der Fall, bei dessen Planung das Konzept "weniger ist mehr" Anwendung findet, wodurch das Projekt durch Stil und Klarheit besticht. Durch die Anordnung mehrerer Baukörper mit klaren geometrischen Strukturen, von denen einige in das Gelände eingebettet und andere durch eine einfache Konstruktion gestützt sind, wird eine formelle Gliederung von Raum und Konstruktion ermöglicht, durch die interessante Effekte zwischen Transparenz und Spiegelung entsteht.

The materials used correspond with the needs of the project. As a result, the proposal of large glazed walls provides an attractive frame surrounding the views over the area.

Le matériel utilisé correspond aux besoins du projet. Dès lors, la présence de grandes surfaces vitrées permet de faire ressortir les vues sur le site.

Der Einsatz der Materialien entspricht den Anforderungen, die bei der Planung des Projektes formuliert wurden. Somit wird den herrlichen Aussichten über die Umgebung durch große Glasflächen ein stilvoller Rahmen verliehen.

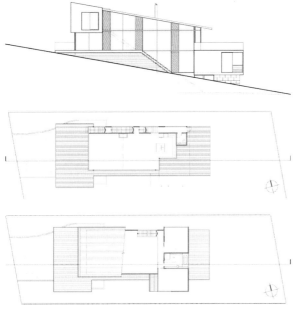

A panoramic view over the surroundings is one of the conditions requested for the project. For this reason the treatment of the spaces is based on their relationship to the area, both physically and visually.

Jouir d'une vue panoramique sur le lieu était l'une des conditions de ce projet. De cette manière, le traitement des espaces est basé sur les relations avec le milieu environnant, aussi bien du point de vue physique que visuel.

Die weiten Aussichten über die Umgebung sind eine der Bedingungen für die Entwicklung des Projektes. Auf diese Weise basiert die räumliche Anordnung auf dem Bezug zum Standort, sowohl physisch als auch optisch gesehen.

MT. MARTHA BEACH HOUSE

Both the spatial proposal and its treatment are directly related to the fact that the house is located on a beach.

L'espace est conçu et exploité suivant l'emplacement particulier de cette maison, sur la plage.

Sowohl die räumliche Anordnung als auch deren Design stehen im direkten Zusammenhang mit dem Standort des Hauses am Strand.

N HOUSE

KAJIMA DESIGN

Tokyo, Japan. 1999-2000

The captivating and unusual characteristics of the terrain where this residence was built were the main conditions determining its design. The lush vegetation surrounding this dwelling –located upon the precipice of Todoroki with a 20 m. drop– makes it difficult to imagine it as situated within the urban area of Tokyo. An enclosed concrete volume containing the service areas was constructed parallel to the street, thus complying with the alignment regulations in the neighbourhood. The residential volume was placed perpendicular to the line of the street and oriented towards the precipice. Its construction in wood and glass takes full advantage of the virtues provided by its natural surroundings.

Les caractéristiques insolites du superbe terrain où cette maison a été construite représentent l'une des principales conditions à prendre en compte pour sa conception. Cette maison se situe au-dessus du précipice de Todoroki, d'une profondeur de 20 m. Avec le paysage luxuriant qui l'entoure, il est difficile d'imaginer que cette habitation se trouve dans la zone urbaine de Tokyo. Parallèlement à la rue, un volume fermé de béton, conforme à l'alignement des maisons du quartier, contient la zone de service. Perpendiculaire à la rue, le volume résidentiel de bois et de verre suit la direction du précipice, et permet de profiter de tous les avantages de l'environnement naturel.

Die wunderschönen und ungewöhnlichen Eigenschaften des Geländes, auf dem dieses Wohnhaus gebaut wird, bilden die Hauptbedingungen, durch die das Design bestimmt wird. Der Standort am 20 m tiefen Abhang von Todoroki wird von einer üppigen Natur umgeben, durch die es schwer ist, sich vorzustellen, dass sich das Haus im Stadtgebiet von Tokio befindet. Parallel zur Strasse wird ein geschlossener Baukörper aus Beton geschaffen, in dem sich die öffentlichen Bereiche befinden und der mit der Ausrichtung des Stadtteils übereinstimmt. Vertikal zum Verlauf der Strasse und zum Abhang hin ausgerichtet befindet sich der Baukörper, der die Wohnbereiche beherbergt. Durch den Einsatz von Holz und Glas wurden die Vorteile der natürlichen Umgebung vollkommen ausgenutzt.

The 455 m². program includes a residence, an office, a reception area for fifty people, guestrooms and a swimming pool.

Cette composition de 455 m² comprend un lieu de vie, un bureau, une salle de réception pour cinquante personnes, des chambres d'amis et une piscine.

Das Programm mit einer Oberfläche von 455 m² schließt eine Wohnung, ein Büro, einen Aufenthaltsraum für fünfzig Personen, Gästezimmer sowie einen Swimmingpool ein.

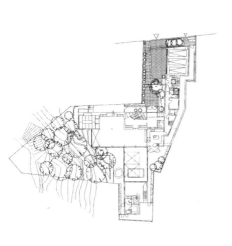

343

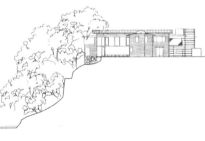

NEW GUILD HOUSE

SETH STEIN ARCHITECTS

London, United Kingdom. 2000

The relationship between spaces and materials is enhanced in the work of Seth Stein through the use of intermediate elements, such as the lighting, which provide attractive formal and spatial solutions to his projects. This house, built in the Notting Hill neighbourhood, uses an architectural form completely unexpected in the region. The shape of the plot, originally a garage, and the creation of a courtyard suggest the arrangement of a part of the proposal. In this manner an L-shaped floor plan is organized about an exterior open air space. A linear spatial sequence facing onto the courtyard throughout its entire length is generated in the longer wing. Formally the house, with its white walls and curved roof, contrasts with the brick architecture typical of the region.

Dans l'œuvre de Seth Stein, la relation entre les espaces et le matériel est enrichie à travers des éléments intermédiaires, comme par exemple la lumière, qui donne à ses projets l'élégance des formes et une répartition spatiale soignée. L'architecture de cette maison est tout à fait insolite à Notting Hill, l'arrondissement où elle se trouve. Les caractéristiques du terrain, – un vieux garage – et la création d'un patio, forment une partie de ce projet. Ainsi, une structure en "L", s'organise autour d'un espace en plein air. Une séquence spatiale linéaire dans l'aile la plus longue s'étend le long du patio. Les formes de cette maison aux murs blancs et au toit incliné créent un contraste avec les bâtiments de briques caractéristiques de la zone.

In dem Werk von Seth Stein wird die Verbindung zwischen Räumen und Materialien durch Zwischenelemente bereichert, wie zum Beispiel durch Licht. Damit werden seinen Projekten stilvolle formelle und räumliche Eigenschaften verliehen. Die Architektur dieses im Stadtteil Notting Hill errichteten Hauses ist in dieser Gegend sehr unüblich. Ein Teil der Planung orientiert sich an der Form des Grundstückes, auf dem sich vorher eine Garage befand. Außerdem soll das Projekt einen Hof beinhalten. Demnach schließt also der Baukörper in L-Form einen Außenraum ohne Überdachung ein. In dem längeren Flügel des Gebäudes wird eine lineare räumliche Sequenz geschaffen, durch die man die Aussicht auf den Hof genießen kann. Der formelle Aspekt des Hauses mit weißen Wänden und einem runden Dach entspricht nicht der typischen Architektur der Gegend, die sich durch den Einsatz von Ziegeln auszeichnet.

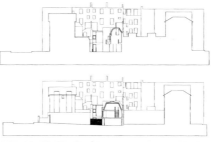

The commission for this new house included a small office. The local regulations permitted construction of up to two floors plus an additional level beneath the curve of the roof.

Le projet de cette nouvelle maison devait inclure un petit bureau. La réglementation de la zone a permis de cons-truire deux niveaux et un supplémentaire qui s'introduit dans le profil incurvé du toit.

Gemäß dem Auftrag zur Errichtung dieses neuen Hauses wird auch ein kleines Büro angeordnet. Den gesetzlichen Regelungen des Standortes entsprechend wird die Errichtung eines zweistöckigen Gebäudes erlaubt, sowie die eines dritten Dachgeschosses mit runder Decke.

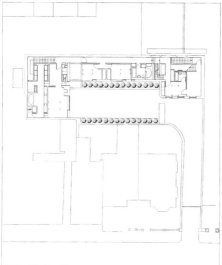

The proposal of a courtyard provides the house with a greater degree of privacy and also permits the introduction of natural light into the spaces.

Le concept du patio permet un degré plus élevé d'intimité dans la maison, tout en laissant entrer le jour dans les différentes pièces.

Durch die Planung eines Hofes wird dem Haus ein höheres Maß an Privatsphäre verliehen, und gleichzeitig fällt in die Räume natürliches Licht ein.

O RESIDENCE

KISHO KUROKAWA ARCHITECT & ASSOCIATES

Tokyo, Japan. 1997-1999

The measurements of the plot where this house is placed, 917 m²., allowed the project to be laid out over different areas. Thus the house consists of three distinct elements: the main building, the area dedicated to the tea ceremony and the bridge which joins the two. This fragmentation of the plan made a careful handling of each of the spaces possible. The area destined for the tea ceremony became a small pavilion whose external image is that of a concrete box containing a wooden building within. The handling of this small reticulate element allows the light to be manipulated according to the needs of the interior.

Les dimensions du terrain où se situe cette maison de 917m² permet son développement sur plusieurs zones. Cet édifice est composé de trois éléments différenciables : la maison principale, une pièce réservée à la cérémonie du thé, et le pont qui les rattache. Cette disposition permet le traitement minutieux de chacun des espaces. La partie destinée à servir le thé se transforme en un petit pavillon dont l'image extérieure est celle d'une caisse de béton, qui renferme une construction en bois. Le traitement de ce petit élément réticulaire permet de manipuler la lumière en fonction des convenances au sein de la maison.

Dieses Haus befindet sich auf einem Grundstück mit einer Oberfläche von 917 m². Dieses Ausmaß ermöglicht die Errichtung des Projekts in verschiedenen Abschnitten. Demnach besteht das Haus aus drei unterschiedlichen Elementen, dem Haupthaus, dem Raum für die Teezeremonie und einer Brücke, durch die sie miteinander verbunden werden. Durch diese Aufteilung des Projektes kann jeder einzelne Bereich detailliert bearbeitet werden. Der Bereich für die Teezeremonie wird zu einem kleinen Pavillon, der von außen wie ein Betonblock wirkt, in seinem Inneren jedoch aus Holz gefertigt ist. Das Design dieses kleinen Pavillons ermöglicht die Nutzung des Lichtes je nach Bedarf im Innenraum.

The main house and the pavilion for the tea ceremony are joined by a bridge with slots along the sides which produce interesting plays of light and introduce an intimate atmosphere which is reinforced upon entering within the area.

La maison principale et le pavillon réservé à la cérémonie du thé sont reliés par un pont strié qui offre de fascinants jeux de lumière et qui instaure une atmosphère d'intimité, renforcée une fois à l'intérieur.

Das Haupthaus und der Pavillon für die Teezeremonie sind durch eine Brücke miteinander verbunden. Die Brückengeländer sind gerillt, wodurch interessante Lichteffekte entstehen, die den Beginn einer behaglichen Atmosphäre einleiten, die innen noch verstärkt wird.

O RESIDENCE

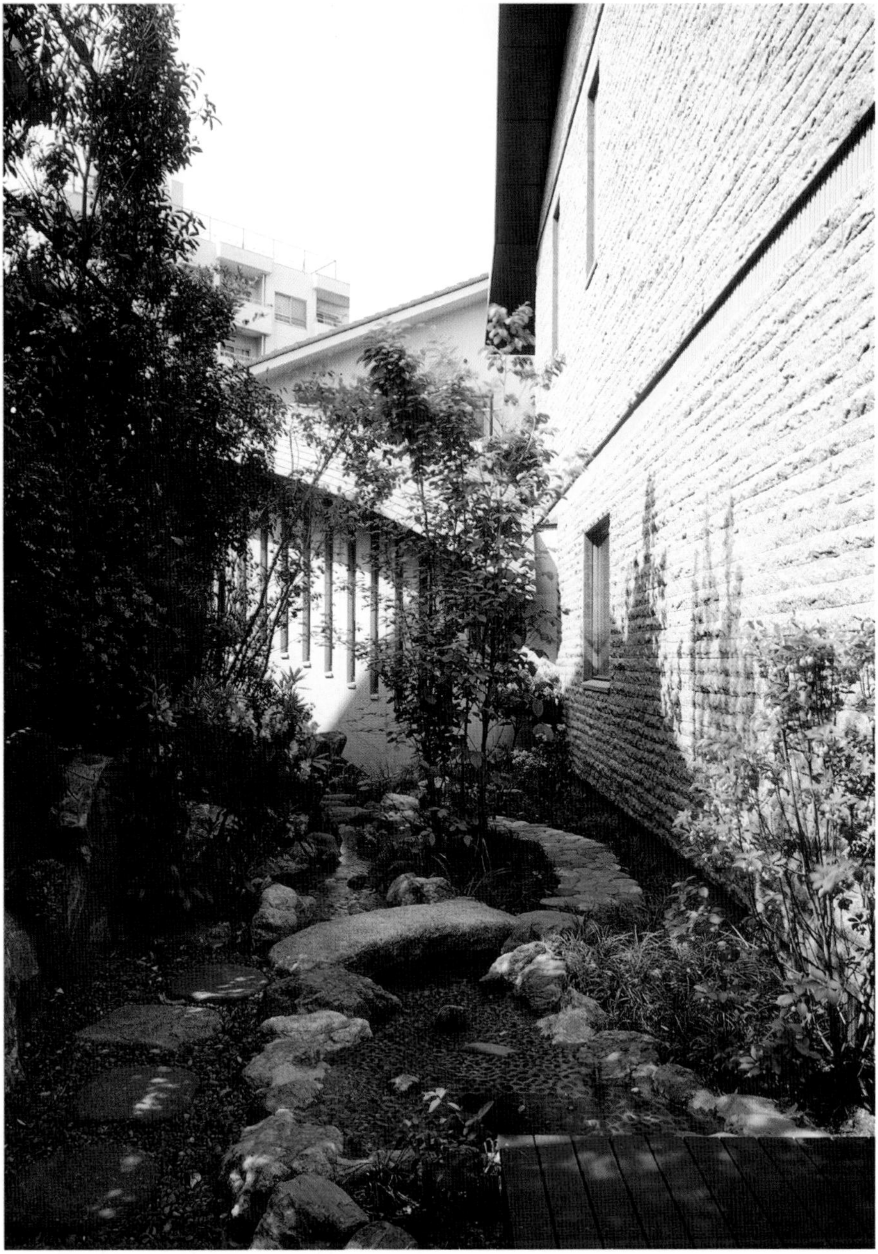

O Residence

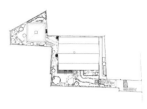

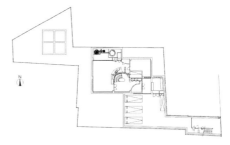

The central tea area is surrounded by a gallery whose walls support 4 of the paintings of the *Water Fall* series by the artist Hirsohi Senju. The permeability of the wooden grid in the internal area allows the paintings to be visible at all times.

La pièce centrale où l'on sert le thé est entourée d'une galerie dont les murs arborent quatre des peintures de la série Water Fall, *de l'artiste Hirsohi Senju. La perméabilité de la réticule de bois à l'intérieur permet d'admirer les peintures à tout moment.*

Der zentrale Bereich für die Teezeremonie ist von einer Galerie umgeben, deren Wände mit vier Bildern der Serie *Water Fall* des Künstlers Hirsohi Senju geschmückt sind. Die Durchlässigkeit der Holzkonstruktion im Innenraum ermöglicht, die Werke immer sehen zu können.

WOHNHAUS PAPST

ERNST GISELBRECHT ARCHITEKT

Steiermark, Österreich. 1993-1995 / 1996

In order to compensate for the unevenness of the terrain, this house was built upon a great platform which fits snugly into the slope. The result of this strategy was the construction of a plane presenting a combination of two possibilities: that of resting upon the terrain and that of "floating" over it. In order to achieve these effects, a forest of *pilotis* was used to keep the platform level. The line of the rooftop, with large eaves reinforcing this horizontal direction, protects a partially-buried three-storey volume. The floor plan of this volume was arranged about a central axis comprising a stairway with bedrooms on either side. Spatially, the platform was transformed into a wide terrace surrounding a part of the residence.

Pour compenser la dénivellation du terrain, cette maison a été construite sur une grande plate-forme qui vient s'emboîter sur la pente. Le résultat est un projet qui allie deux possibilités : s'appuyer sur le terrain et "flotter" au dessus de celui-ci. Pour y parvenir, un bois de pilotis se charge de maintenir la plateforme horizontale. En outre, la ligne du toit, avec de grands avant-toits, protège un volume de trois étages partiellement enseveli. L'escalier forme l'axe central qui organise la structure, avec des chambres de chaque côté. Du point de vue de l'espace, la plateforme s'élargit pour devenir une grande terrasse qui entoure une partie de l'habitation.

Um sich an die Neigung des Geländes anzupassen, wurde das Haus auf einer großen Plattform errichtet, die sich in den Abhang eingliedert. Daher werden im Grundriss zwei Möglichkeiten miteinander kombiniert. Zum einen wird sich auf das Gelände gestützt und zum anderen soll das Haus über ihm "schweben". Um dies zu erreichen, wird die horizontale Plattform durch einen Wald von Streben gestützt. Diese Horizontalität wird durch die Anordnung des Daches mit großflächigen Flügeln unterstützt, durch das der dreistöckige teilweise in das Gelände einschneidende Baukörper geschützt wird. Der Grundriss basiert auf einer zentralen Achse, die durch die eine Treppe gebildet wird, zu deren Seiten sich die Zimmer befinden. Die Plattform wird in räumlicher Hinsicht zu einer weiträumigen Terrasse, von der ein Teil des Wohnhauses umgeben wird.

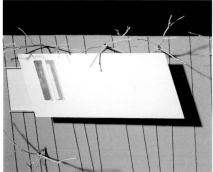

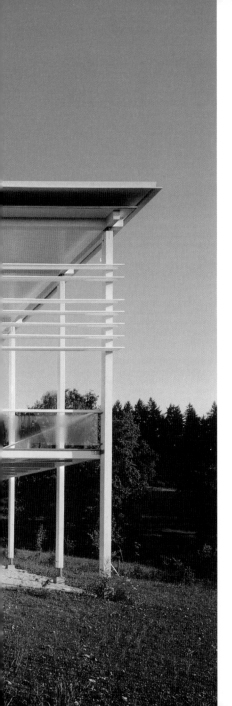

The project was based upon two horizontal planes, the terrace and the roof, which contain a blank three-storey volume. The protection provided by the eaves on the rooftop permits the introduction of great windows onto the façades.

Le projet est basé sur deux plans horizontaux, la terrasse et le toit, qui contiennent un volume blanc à trois niveaux. Les avants-toits servent de protection à la structure, ce qui permet l'insertion de grandes baies vitrées dans les façades.

Das Projekt basiert auf zwei horizontal angeordneten Grundrissen, der Terrasse und dem Dach, die durch einen weißen dreistöckigen Baukörper verbunden werden. Durch den Schutz, der durch die Flügel des Daches geboten wird, können an den Fassaden große Fenster angeordnet werden.

WOHNHAUS PAPST

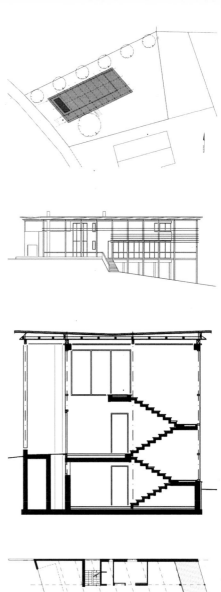

WOHNHAUS PAPST

HOUSE IN THE PERIFERY

WALLACE CUNINGHAM

California, USA. 1991

The design of this house is based on a pattern of longitudinal bands creeping over the terrain little by little. The placement of each of these bands within the composition, nonetheless, permits great formal and spatial variety. Thus, the width, length and height of the bands provide for a large number of possible situations: from interior courtyards to skylights. The design of the façade clearly reflects the longitudinal nature of the proposal. Parallel planes of differing heights provide order to the structure of the volume "using lines". Apart from this arrangement, the interior spaces have been organized freely within the given plan.

Un schéma de bandes longitudinales forme le concept de cette maison, occupant successivement le terrain. Toutefois, la disposition de chacune d'entre elles à l'intérieur de la composition offre une grande variété formelle et spatiale. Ainsi, la longueur, largeur et hauteur des bandes permettent d'obtenir une multitude de situations, de patios intérieurs jusqu'à la projection zénithale de la lumière. La conception des façades reflète clairement le modèle longitudinal. Des plans parallèles à différentes hauteurs organisent une volumétrie "de lignes" à l'intérieur de l'ensemble. Outre cet agencement, les pièces de la maison s'organisent librement dans ce schéma.

Das Design dieses Hauses beruht auf einer schematischen Anordnung von linienförmigen Umrandungen, durch die das Gelände nach und nach bedeckt wird. Durch die Anordnung jeder einzelnen in der Gestaltung des Gesamtwerkes wird eine große formelle und räumliche Vielfalt ermöglicht. Somit wird durch die Breite, die Länge oder die Höhe dieser Umrandungen die Vielfalt zwischen den verschiedenen Bereichen geschaffen, angefangen bei Innenhöfen bis hin zu beleuchteten Zeniteingängen. Durch die Gestaltung der Fassaden kommt die längliche Planung deutlich zum Ausdruck. Die durch Linien angeordnete Volumetrie des Gesamtwerkes wird durch zueinander parallel angeordnete Flächen auf verschiedenen Höhen organisiert. Ganz unabhängig davon werden die Innenräume in diesem Schema sehr frei angeordnet.

The variations presented in the lengths of the different bands make it possible to alternate interior and exterior spaces, which produces an exceptional spatial composition.

La variété dans la longueur des bandes permet d'alterner espaces intérieurs et extérieurs, ce qui donne comme résultat une intéressante composition spatiale.

Durch die Längenvielfalt der einzelnen Umrandungen werden die Innenräume mit den äußeren Bereichen verbunden, wodurch eine interessante räumliche Anordnung entsteht.

HAUS R128

WERNER SOBEK INGENIEURE

Stuttgart, Deutschland. 1997 / 1999-2000

This residence located on the hills of Stuttgart is built on a narrow plot with a difficult access. Its characteristics forced the project to be planned with a constructive commitment which would facilitate carrying out the work while at the same time enjoying the charms of the location. In addition to this the designer –owner of the lot– wished to develop the virtues of an ecological and recyclable house. After a process questioning the current construction methods, an elegant glass cube, which can be entered by crossing a bridge, was built. Its geometric logic permitted the prefabrication and standardization of the constructive elements which are in addition recyclable.

Cette demeure, située sur les collines de Stuttgart, est bâtie sur un terrain étroit et difficile d'accès. Ses caractéristiques rendent indispensable un compromis constructif pour faciliter la mise en œuvre et permettre de tirer profit des charmes de ce lieu. En outre son auteur – et propriétaire – souhaitait exploiter les avantages d'une maison écologique et recyclable. Après une procédure qui consiste à réimplanter les formes actuelles de construction, on aménage un élégant cube de verre, auquel on accède par un pont, et dont la logique géométrique permet la préfabrication et standardisation des éléments de construction qui sont de plus recyclables.

Dieses Wohnhaus, das sich auf den Stuttgarter Hügeln befindet, wurde auf einem engen Grundstück mit schwierigem Zugang gebaut. Aufgrund der Beschaffenheit des Standortes musste bei der Entwicklun des Projekts speziell berücksichtigt werden, die Bauarbeiten zu erleichtern und gleichzeitig die Vorzüge des Standortes auszunutzen. Außerdem war es für den Architekten und Eigentümer von Priorität, die Vorteile eines ökologischen und wieder verwertbaren Hauses zu entwickeln. Nach einem Prozess, in dem die aktuellen Bauformen neu konzipiert werden, wird ein stilvoller Glaswürfel gebaut, zu dem man über eine Brücke gelangt, dessen geometrische Logik die Vorfertigung und Normung der Bauelemente ermöglicht, die außerdem wieder verwertbar sind.

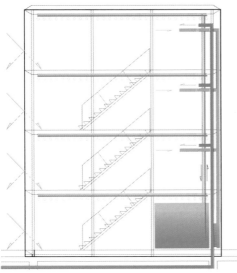

The need for transparency both in the interior as well as in the exterior allows each of the 4 floors of the building to require only the minimum amount of furnishings necessary to define each area.

Dû au besoin de transparence aussi bien à l'intérieur qu'à l'extérieur, le minimum de mobilier nécessaire est utilisé dans les quatre niveaux de la maison, délimitant ainsi chacun des espaces.

Aufgrund des Bedarfs an äußerer und innerer Transparenz wurden die vier Etagen des Wohnhauses mit einem Minimum an notwendigem Mobiliar eingerichtet, um jedem einzelnen Raum sein Ambiente zu geben.

HAUS R128

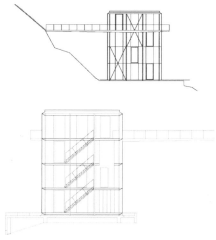

The house was designed as a completely recyclable and self-sufficient building in terms of its systems of climate control. Thus all the energy is absorbed from the sun, stored and used according to climatic necessities.

Ce logement a été conçu comme un bâtiment entièrement recyclable et autosuffisant quant aux systèmes de climatisation. Ainsi, toute l'énergie solaire est absorbée pour ensuite s'accumuler et s'utiliser en fonction des besoins climatiques.

Das Haus wurde als komplett wieder verwertbares und sparsames Gebäude entworfen, was die Systeme zur Regulierung der Innentemperatur betrifft. Somit wird Sonnenenergie absorbiert, gespeichert und je nach klimatischen Bedingungen verwendet.

CASA ROJAS

LUIS IZQUIERDO, ANTONIA LEHMANN

Santiago de Chile, Chile. 1998-2000

The parcelling out of the land in several residential development projects limits the formal possibilities of these projects to houses facing street and garden. As a result, in many cases the decision is made to close off the street side of the projects, to the extent that in some cases the structure of the house might become completely concealed from the exterior. In the case of this residence as well, located in the La Dehesa Valley, the need to close itself off from the street is the decisive factor in the project. Nonetheless, the element which in other homes is presented as a blank wall, becomes, in this project, an attractive proposal for a mixture of walls interacting with closed structures in order to create a play of light and shadow.

Souvent, le parcellement de complexes résidentiels limite les possibilités formelles des projets dont le jardin donne sur la rue. En conséquence, on opte dans de nombreux cas pour la fermeture de l'habitation à la rue, ce qui parfois masque complètement la volumétrie de la maison. C'est le cas de cette maison qui se trouve dans la vallée de La Dehesa, où le besoin d'être fermé à la rue constitue en partie l'organisation du projet. Cependant, ce qui dans certaines maisons est un mur aveugle, forme ici un ensemble attrayant de plans qui agissent de concert avec les volumétries fermées pour créer un effet de lumières et d'ombres.

Die Parzellierung vieler Wohnungsbauprojekte grenzt die formellen Möglichkeiten der Projekte insofern ein, dass die Frontseite entweder zur Strasse oder zum Garten hin ausgerichtet werden kann. Daher wurde in vielen Fällen entschlossen, die Projekte zur Strasse zu schließen, wodurch mitunter die Volumetrie des Hauses komplett versteckt wird. Dieses Wohnhaus, das sich in Valle de La Dehesa befindet, schließt sich ebenfalls der Strasse, die einen Teil des Projektes bildet. Was für einige Häuser jedoch eine blinde Mauer ist, ist hier eine attraktive Anordnung von zueinander versetzten Flächen, die mit geschlossenen Volumetrien zueinander in Beziehung stehen, wodurch angenehme Licht-Schatten-Effekte entstehen.

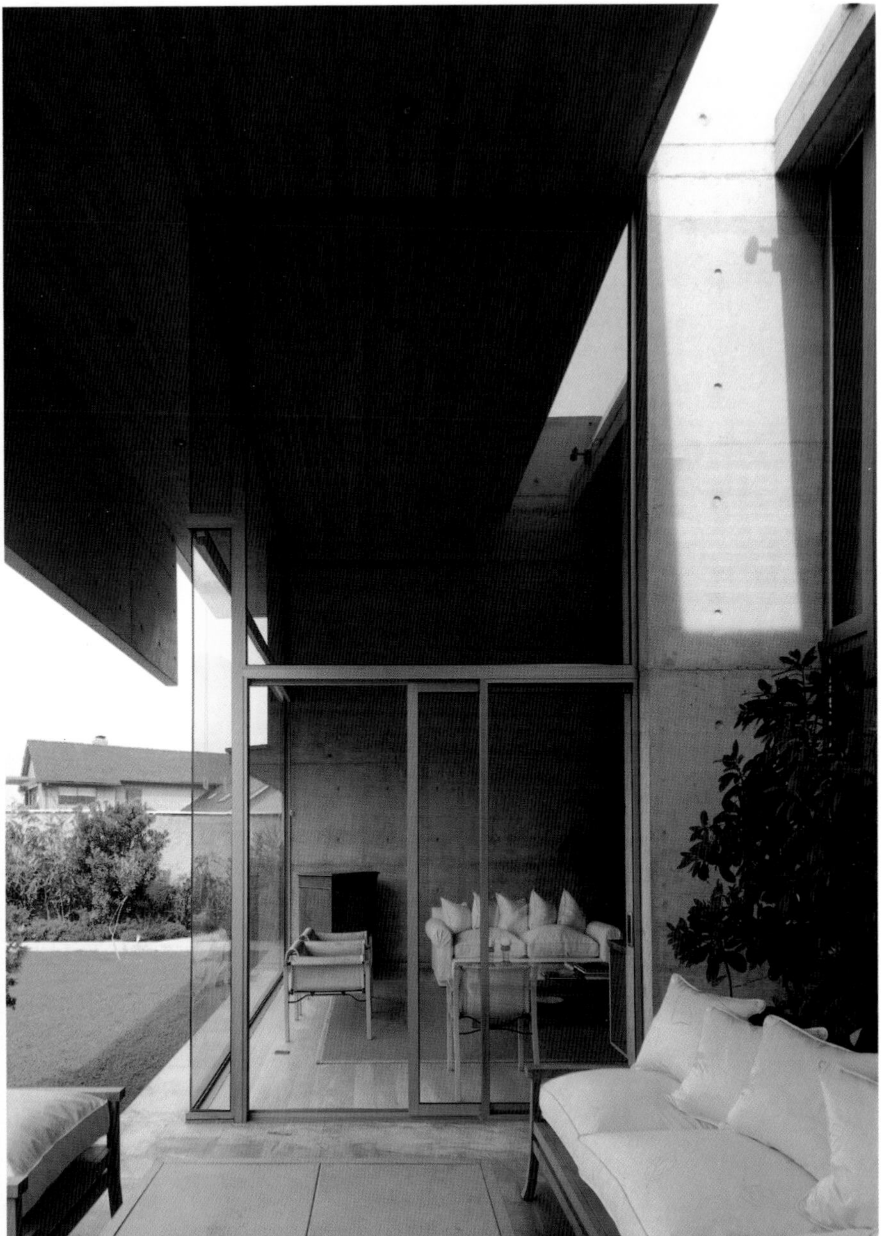

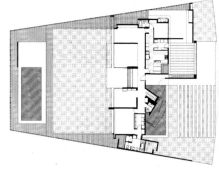

The proposal for the house is organized as an ensemble completely closed off to the street and open towards the large back garden.

La maison est organisée comme un ensemble entièrement fermé à la rue et ouvert sur un grand jardin à l'arrière.

Das Hauses wird als zur Strasse vollständig geschlossenes und zum hinteren Garten geöffnetes Projekt entworfen.

Sagaponac House N° 22

Eric Owen Moss Architects

New York, USA. 2000-2003

Using pure objects, Eric Owen Moss has developed complex formal proposals which nonetheless preserve the geometric coherence which organizes the structure and its areas with ease during development of the project. This house is a clear example of this type of proposal. Its structure is the result of two elements: a uniform "box" with straight lines and a "cord" which encircles it and compresses it gradually. As a result of this process the centre box narrows in the middle and widens out at both ends, the surfaces become warped, straight lines become twisted. Nevertheless the initial structure remains recognizable even during the final stage of the project.

Eric Owen Moss développe à partir d'objets purs des propositions formelles complexes qui maintiennent la cohérence géométrique qui permet d'organiser aisément la structure et les espaces pendant la construction. Cette maison est un parfait exemple de ce type de projets. Sa volumétrie est la combinaison de deux éléments : une "caisse" régulière aux lignes droites et une "corde" qui l'entoure et la compresse peu à peu. En conséquence, la caisse centrale se rétrécit au centre et s'élargit sur les côtés ; les surfaces se gondolent, les lignes droites se tordent... et pourtant, le volume initial reste reconnaissable dans ce projet toujours en phase finale.

Auf puren Objekten basierend werden von Eric Owen Moss komplexe formelle Planungen entwikkelt, in denen die jedoch die Kohärenz der Geometrie erhalten bleibt, durch die in der Entwicklungsphase des Projektes die strukturelle und räumliche Anordnung erleichtert wird. Dieses Haus ist ein klares Beispiel für diese Planungsweise. Zwei Elemente machen seine Volumetrie aus: ein gewöhnlicher "Block" mit geraden Linien, umgeben von einer "Schnur", durch die er nach und nach komprimiert wird. Dieser Prozess führt zu einer Verengung des zentralen Kastens im mittleren Teil und zu einer Erweiterung an den Enden, wobei die Oberflächen gekrümmt und die geraden Linien gebogen werden... trotzdem ist der ursprüngliche Baukörper sogar noch in der Schlußphase des Projektes noch erkennbar.

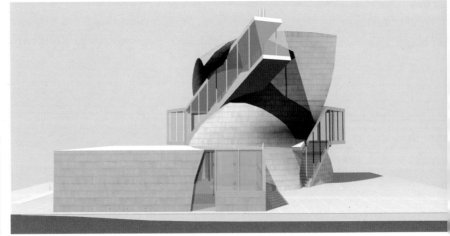

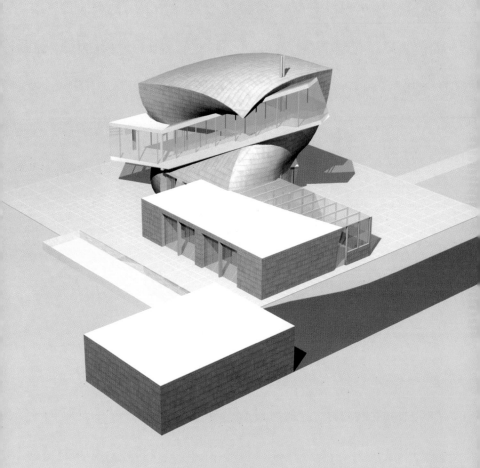

What is initially a "cord" in the geometric study becomes, on the floor plan, a stairway which encircles the central structure and facilitates communication between the different levels of the house.

Ce qui dans l'étude géométrique est une "corde" devient dans la conception un escalier qui entoure le volume central et dont le rôle est de relier tous les niveaux de la maison entre eux.

Was aus geometrischer Sicht eine "Schnur" ist, wird im Projekt zu einer Treppe, die um den zentralen Baukörper führt und alle Etagen des Hauses miteinander verbindet.

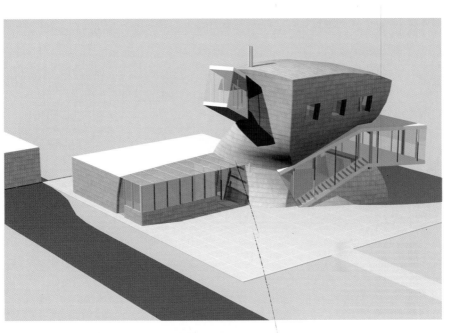

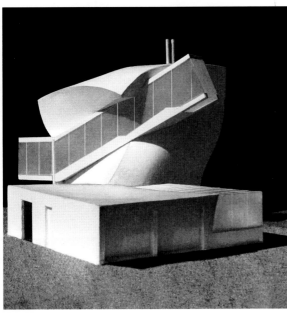

SAGAPONAC HOUSE Nº 22

Casa en Santa Margarita

Ángel Sánchez-Cantalejo / Vicente Tomás

Sta. Margarita, Mallorca. 1997 / 1999-2001

This residence situated on the crest of a hill can be found at the edge of the urban limits of the town; this fact imbues the house with a noticeable mixture of urban and rural characteristics, which have been reinforced from the beginning of the project: a great concrete wall, which is opened only to allow access to the building, clearly defines its boundaries. The house was placed at one end of the plot allowing for the development of an attractive sequence of exterior spaces. The formal image of the estate is provided by only two elements: a "box" covered with wood resting upon three structural concrete walls.

L'emplacement de cette maison en haut d'une colline, à proximité du centre d'un village, lui confère un caractère limitrophe accentué entre cadre urbain et rural. Cette qualité est renforcée par la présence d'un grand mur de béton qui marque nettement la frontière, ne s'ouvrant que pour permettre l'accès à la maison. Etabli à l'extrémité du terrain, le bâtiment comprend une intéressante séquence d'espaces extérieurs. Deux éléments seulement donnent l'image formelle de l'ensemble : un "caisson" de bois, et les trois murs structuraux en béton sur lesquels il repose.

Das auf einem Hügel errichtete Wohnhaus befindet sich am Rande des Stadtkerns, was ihm den markanten Charakter der Grenze zwischen dem Städtischen und dem Ländlichen verleiht. Durch eine hohe Betonmauer wird deutlich die Grenze des Hauses gekennzeichnet, die sich nur dem Zugang zur Wohnung öffnet. Das Haus wurde an einem Ende des Grundstückes errichtet, wodurch eine interessante räumliche Sequenz der äußeren Bereiche ermöglicht wird. Das formelle Bild des Gesamtwerkes wird nur durch zwei Elemente gebildet. Ein mit Holz verkleideter "Block", der auf drei strukturelle Betonmauern gestützt ist.

Placing the dwelling at one end of the plot made it possible to organize a series of exterior spaces with different characters and measurements. Collaboration in landscape architecture was provided by Bet Figueras.

L'emplacement de la maison sur l'une des extrémités du terrain permet d'organiser les espaces extérieurs aux caractéristiques et dimensions variées. L'œuvre a bénéficié de la collaboration de l'architecte Bet Figueras, qui propose une architecture paysagiste.

Durch die Positionierung des Wohnhauses an einem Ende des Grundstückes können die äußeren Bereiche nach verschiedenen Charakteristika und Abmessungen angeordnet werden. Die Mitarbeit der Landschaftsarchitektur wurde durch die Architektin Bet Figueras organisiert.

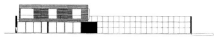

The way in which the materials –concrete, wood and glass– are used reinforces the innate character of each of these materials: solidity, lightness and fragility.

La forme des matériaux utilisés – béton, bois et verre – rehausse le caractère intrinsèque de chacun d'entre eux : solidité, légèreté et fragilité.

Durch die Art des Einsatzes der Materialien Beton, Holz und Glas wird der wesentliche Charakter jedes einzelnen, Beständigkeit, Leichtigkeit und Zerbrechlichkeit, verstärkt.

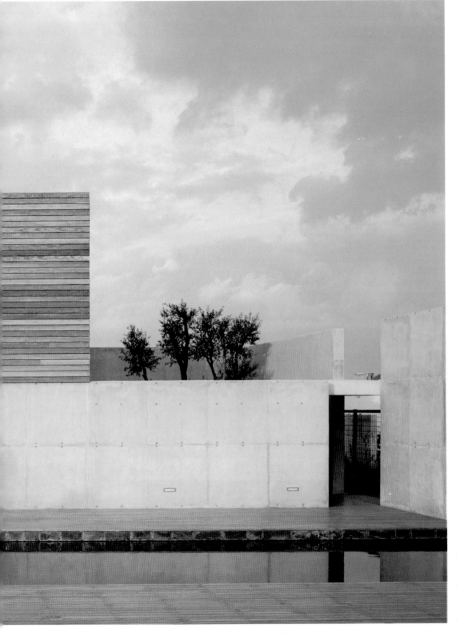

CASA EN SANTA MARGARITA

SANTO OVIDIO ESTATE

ÁLVARO SIZA, ARQUITECTO

Portugal. 1995-1999

This project demonstrates once again the virtuosity of the architecture of Alvaro Siza, who achieves enormous spatial and formal quality in his work starting with a careful study of the local conditions and a detailed development of the project. This project belonging to a large agricultural and forest centre, consisted of the overall recovery and restoration of the entire area. In the main house, with two floors originally separated from one another, all the spaces were recovered in order to facilitate a unitary functioning. Old outbuildings were integrated into the main nucleus, thus making it possible to propose an indoor swimming pool as well as the recovery of spaces which had become lost such as the chapel dedicated to Saint Ovidio.

Ce projet démontre une fois de plus le talent de l'architecte Alvaro Siza, qui parvient, grâce à l'étude minutieuse des conditions environnantes et une élaboration détaillée du projet, à réaliser des œuvres de grande qualité tant au niveau des formes que de l'espace. Ce projet, qui fait partie d'un grand centre agricole et forestier, consiste à reprendre en main et à rénover la propriété. Dans la maison principale, constituée de deux niveaux jusqu'alors séparés, tous les espaces sont utilisés afin d'obtenir un fonctionnement unitaire. De vieilles dépendances s'unissent au noyau principal, ce qui laisse de l'espace libre en prévision d'une piscine couverte ou de fonctions pendant longtemps inutilisées comme la chapelle dédiée à Santo Ovidio.

Dieses Projekt ist eines vieler Beispiele für die architektonische Fertigkeit von Alvaro Siza, dessen Werke, ausgehend von einer genauen Studie der Beschaffenheit der Umgebung und einer detaillierten Projektentwicklung, durch hohe räumliche und formelle Qualität bestechen. Im Rahmen dieses Projektes soll ein großes land- und forstwirtschaftliches Gelände rundum saniert werden. Im zweistöckigen Haupthaus, dessen Etagen vorher voneinander getrennt waren, werden alle Bereiche miteinander verbunden, um somit einen einheitlichen Betrieb zu gewährleisten. Vorherige Abschnitte werden an das zentrale Hauptgebäude angeschlossen, wodurch die Schaffung eines überdachten Swimmingpools oder die Nutzung zusätzlicher Räumlichkeiten ermöglicht wird, wie zum Beispiel die Kapelle Sto. Ovidio.

The materials used were granite and zinc for the exterior, marble, wood and ceramic tiles for the interior areas.

Les matériaux utilisés sont le granit et le zinc pour l'extérieur, et le marbre, bois et carreaux dans la maison.

Die eingesetzten Materialien sind Granit und Zink für die Außenbereiche und Marmor, Holz und Fliesen für die Innenräume.

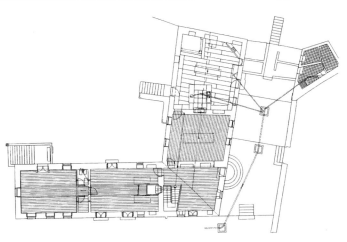

The reconstruction of the garden and the exterior spaces permitted the recovery of important elements in the area, such as the belvedere and the pergola.

Les transformations dans le jardin et les espaces extérieurs permettent de récupérer les éléments importants de l'œuvre comme le belvédère ou la pergola.

Durch den Bezug zum Garten und zu den äußeren Bereichen werden bedeutende Elemente des Gesamten erschlossen, wie zum Beispiel die Pergola.

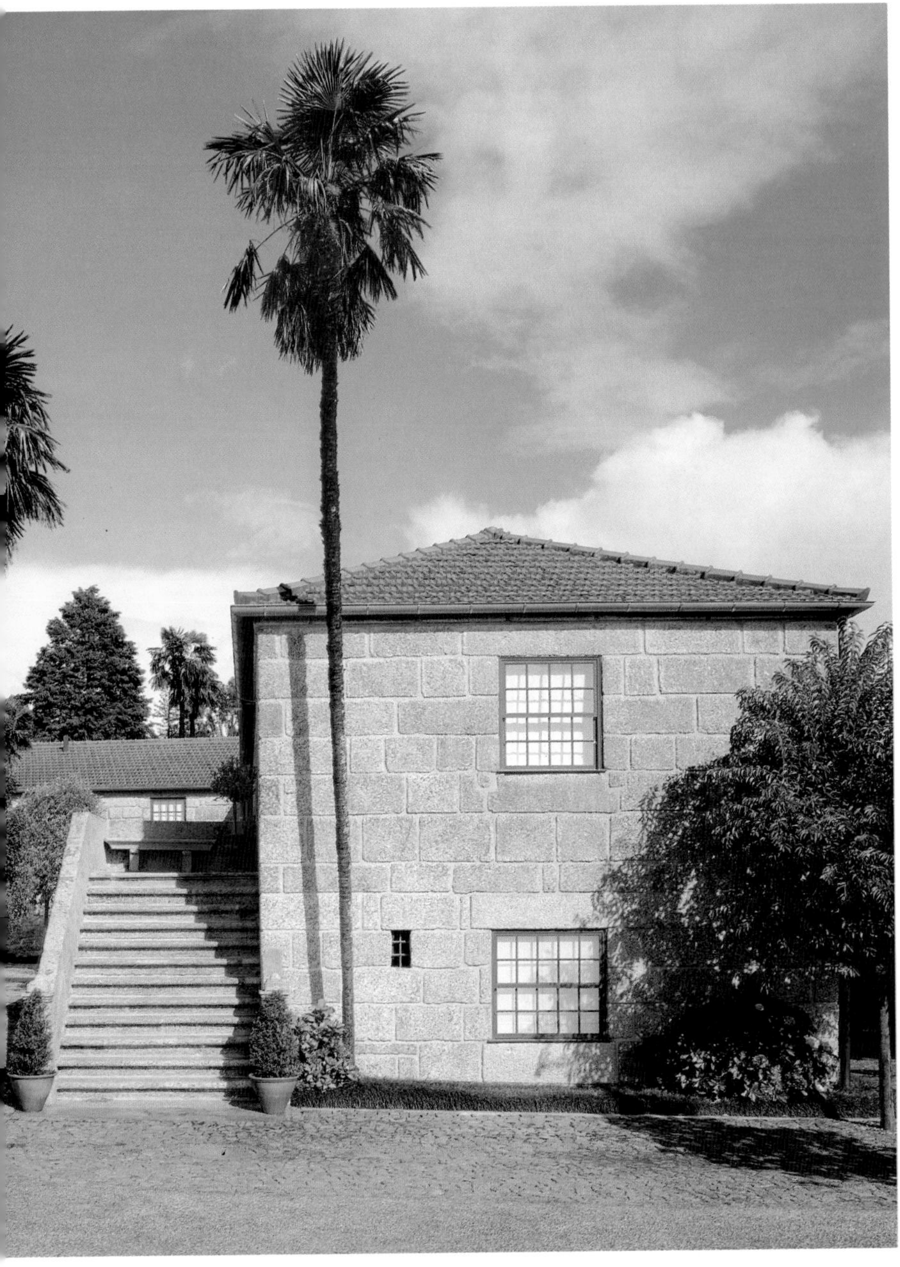

Santo Ovidio Estate

SEKINE DENTAL CLINIC AND RESIDENCE

EDWARD SUZUKI ASSOCIATES

Saitama Prefecture, Japan. 2001

Many of the works of this designer investigate the theme concerning the possibilities of dual concepts in a project. Thus closely-related dialectics are generated between the ideas of open-closed, exterior-interior. This tendency can be verified in this project for a residence and dental clinic. The formal image of the ensemble is provided by a circle of perforated sheet metal, which nonetheless "hides" and protects a form with straight lines. The contrast between these two shapes, where the circle acts as a "skin", allows for the creation of intermediate spaces which become green areas and act as acoustic and visual protection for the inside activities.

Nombreuses des œuvres de cet auteur tournent autour des possibilités de doubles concepts au sein d'un même projet. Dès lors, des dialectiques étroites se créent entre ouvert et fermé, intérieur et extérieur, etc. Cet objectif est concrétisé dans ce projet d'habitation et de clinique dentaire. Un cercle de tôle d'acier perforée donne l'image formelle de l'ensemble, tout en "cachant" et protégeant une géométrie de lignes droites. Le contraste entre ces deux formes, où le cercle sert de couche protectrice, permet de créer des éléments intermédiaires qui deviennent des espaces verts et agissent comme les protections acoustiques et visuelles de l'activité intérieure.

In vielen Werken dieses Architekten werden die Möglichkeiten dualer Konzepte in einem Projekt erforscht. Auf diese Weise wird eine enge Dialektik zwischen offen – geschlossen oder außen– innen geschaffen... In diesem Projekt für eine Wohnung und eine Zahnklinik kann diese Tendenz bestätigt werden. Die formelle Gestaltung des Gesamtwerkes besteht aus einem Ring aus perforiertem Metallblech, der die Geometrie gerader Linien "verstecken" und schützen soll. Durch die beiden Formen entsteht ein Kontrast, wobei der Ring als Schutzschicht dient. Auf diese Weise werden Zwischenräume geschaffen, die als Grünflächen gestaltet werden und als akustischer und optischer Schutz der Innenräume dienen.

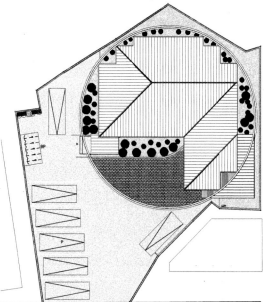

The circle which protects the inner area is of sheet metal and its structure is independent from that of the internal volume. The "residual" space between the two shapes creates a green cushion which protects the privacy of the inside activities.

Le cercle qui protège la géométrie intérieure est formé de tôle, et sa structure est indépendante du volume intérieur. Les espaces "restants" entre les deux formes donnent naissance à un matelas de verdure qui préserve l'intimité intérieure.

Der Ring, durch den die inneren Formen geschützt werden, ist aus Metallblech und seine Struktur ist unabhängig von der des inneren Baukörpers. Die "übrigen" Bereiche zwischen den beiden Elementen bilden eine Grünfläche, durch welche die Privatsphäre der Innenräume bewahrt wird.

This project with a total of 218 m². accommodates a dental clinic of 111 m². on the first floor and a residence on the second floor.

Ce projet de 218m² au total comprend une clinique dentaire de 111m² en bas, et une résidence au premier étage.

Dieses Projekt mit einer Gesamtoberfläche von 218 m² beherbergt in der ersten Etage eine Zahnklinik von 111 m² und eine Wohnung in der zweiten Etage.

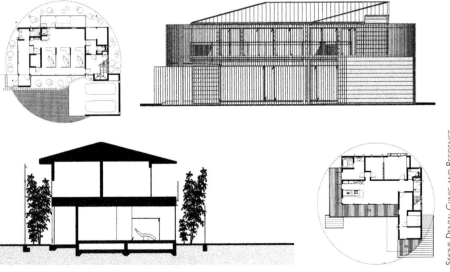

CASA NA SERRA DA ARRÁBIDA

EDUARDO SOUTO DE MOURA

Serra da Arrábida, Portugal. 1994 / 2002

This project has become the "artificial element" which prolongs a part of the terrain in a natural fashion, while at the same time forming an abrupt interruption dividing two different levels on the plot. From the upper level, the structural configuration of the house is only hinted at, allowing for an uninterrupted view over the residence. Nevertheless, the entire structure can be distinguished from the lower level. The design using pure shapes and wide openings generates an attractive balance within the building. The different volumes used in the composition make it possible to define the spaces of the program clearly, both formally and planimetrically.

Ce projet représente l'"élément artificiel" qui prolonge de forme naturelle une partie du terrain pour ensuite marquer la coupure abrupte entre deux pentes. Du niveau le plus élevé, seule la configuration volumétrique de la maison est suggérée, ce qui permet une continuité visuelle sur cette dernière. Une fois en bas, cependant, on peut contempler la volumétrie entière. Le travail des formes pures et les grandes ouvertures donnent du charme et de l'équilibre à l'ensemble. Aussi bien du point de vue des formes que de la planimétrie, les différents volumes utilisés dans la compostion permettent de définir nettement chaque pièce de la maison.

Dieses Projekt wird zu einem "künstlichen Element", durch das ein Teil des Grundstücks auf natürliche Weise verlängert wird und ein abrupter Schnitt zwischen den zwei unterschiedlichen Höhen des Grundstücks entsteht. Auf dem höheren Abschnitt des Grundstücks werden von nur einem Baukörper aus die Aussichten über die Umgebung genutzt, während von dem unteren Abschnitt aus die Volumetrie als einheitlich wahrgenommen wird. Durch die Anordnung klarer Formen und großer Öffnungen wird dem Gesamtwerk ein stilvolles Gleichgewicht verliehen. Durch die formelle Gestaltung und die Planimetrie werden die Bereiche des Projektes klar abgegrenzt.

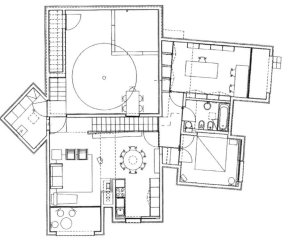

The lengthy process of this project initiated a crisis in the adoption of the design. Nevertheless, once the problems derived from this commission were resolved, the project continued to a successful finale.

A cause du long processus de construction, le schéma sélectionné a été compromis. Une fois les problèmes résolus, cependant, le projet a pu acquérir une solide continuité.

Durch die lange Zeit, die die Planung des Projektes in Anspruch nahm, war man sich über das verwendete Schema nicht sicher. Nachdem jedoch die Probleme des Auftrages gelöst wurden, wurde eine treffende Kontinuität im Projekt erreicht.

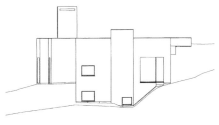

The design with pure volumes into which large, controlled openings are introduced produces a fascinating formal interplay.

Le travail des volumétries pures qui acceuillent de grandes ouvertures contrôlées donne naissance à un intéressant jeu des formes.

Durch die Anordnung klarer Volumetrien, in denen große Öffnungen angeordnet sind, wird eine interessante formelle Gestaltung ermöglicht.

SHENTON PARK RESIDENCE

CRAIG STEERE ARCHITECTS

Shenton Park, Australia. 2002

The views over Shenton Park Lake bestowed upon this location suggested taking maximum advantage of this circumstance right from the beginning of the project, without neglecting the need for privacy inherent to a residence. In addition to this condition, the characteristics of the program required the inclusion of an art gallery. For this reason the architectural proposal began with a close study of this particular situation. The result is a simple composition with a rectangular floor plan and a structure of orthogonal lines, which provide the residence with a sober image.

Les vues sur le lac de Shenton Park suggèrent, dès le début du projet, l'utilisation optimale de cette caractéristique, sans perdre de vue le besoin intrinsèque d'intimité dans une maison. En outre, le projet devait comprendre une galerie d'art, d'où une proposition architecturale basée sur une relation étroite avec ses conditions particulières. Nous nous trouvons ainsi face à une composition simple, avec un plan rectangulaire et une volumétrie de lignes orthogonales qui donnent une image sobre à l'ensemble.

Die Aussichten über den See des *Shenton Park*, die von diesem Standort aus geboten werden, geben bei der Planung dieses Projektes Anlass zur maximalen Nutzung dieser Bedingung, ohne jedoch den Bedarf an Privatsphäre, die in einem Wohnhaus bewahrt werden sollte, aus den Augen zu verlieren. Weiterhin wird gemäß der Eigenschaften des Programmes eine Galerie errichtet, wodurch eine enge Beziehung der architektonischen Planung zu den individuellen Bedingungen entsteht. Folglich wird dem Gesamtwerk durch eine einfache Anordnung mit einer rechteckigen Planimetrie und einer Volumetrie orthogonal angeordneter Linien ein schlichter Eindruck verliehen.

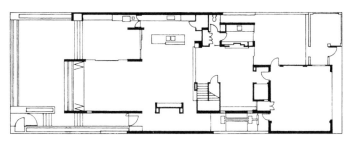

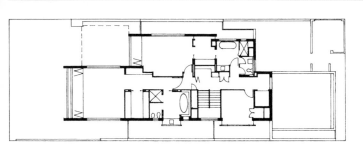

The client desired a house with "modern" lines, easy to maintain and appropriately placed within the context of a nature reserve.

Le client souhaitait une maison aux lignes "modernes", facile à entretenir et bien intégrée à l'environnement du parc naturel.

Nach Wunsch des Auftraggebers sollte das Haus ein modernes Design haben, leicht zu nutzen sein und sich angemessen in die Umgebung des Naturparks eingliedern lassen.

Shiga Residence

Edward Suzuki Associates

Tokyo, Japan. 2001

Enjoying the exterior areas while attempting to fuse them with the interior is one of the most attractive spatial conceptions which can be accomplished in a residence. This intention is clearly visible in this project. The favourable location of this house allowed for the projection of a large terrace along the entire length of the southern façade. Thus the borders between covered and exposed areas become vague, transforming the openings into great sliding doors which provide the possibility of including the terrace as if it were an interior space. In this manner the terrace becomes an intermediate area between the interior and the exterior.

L'utilisation des espaces extérieurs en fusion avec l'intérieur est l'un des concepts spatiaux les plus fascinants que l'on peut trouver dans une habitation ; dans ce projet, l'intention d'y parvenir est nettement visible. L'emplacement favorable de la maison permet l'extension d'une immense terrasse le long de la façade sud. Les limites entre espaces couverts et découverts sont réduites : les embrasures se transforment en grandes portes coulissantes qui peuvent accueillir la terrasse comme un élément intérieur, la convertissant ainsi en un espace intermédiaire entre l'intérieur et l'extérieur.

Der Genuss der äußeren Umgebung durch den Versuch, sie mit dem Innenraum in Bezug zu setzen, ist eines der attraktivsten Raumkonzepte, das in einer Wohnung entwickelt werden kann. In diesem Projekt ist diese Absicht deutlich erkennbar. Der vorteilhafte Standort des Hauses erlaubt die Planung einer großen Terrasse entsprechend der gesamten Länge der südlichen Fassade. Somit verlaufen die Übergänge zwischen überdachten und freien Bereichen. Die Öffnungen sind große Schiebetüren, durch die die Terrasse wie ein Innenraum angeschlossen wird, was sie zu einem Übergangsbereich zwischen innen und außen umwandelt.

In the seasons when the weather permits, the inhabitants can open wide the great windows which protect the interior, thus "containing" the outside spaces through the mediation of the terrace.

Lorsque la température le permet, les occupants de cette résidence peuvent ouvrir entièrement les baies vitrées qui protègent l'intérieur, ce qui permet de "contenir" l'espace extérieur par le biais de la terrasse.

In den Jahreszeiten mit vorteilhaften klimatischen Bedingungen können die Bewohner die großen Panoramafenster, die den Innenraum abgrenzen, komplett öffnen und somit durch die Terrasse die äußeren Bereiche "einbeziehen".

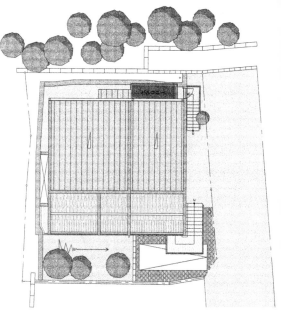

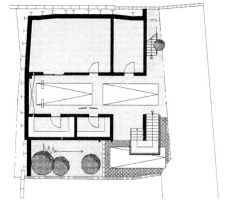

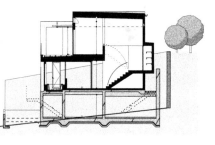

SPANISH HOUSE

KISHO KUROKAWA ARCHITECT & ASSOCIATES

Menorca, España. 1996

This house, which has not been built, was destined to be placed on a hillside by the seashore, which would have provided the project with privileged views. This attractive location appeared to suggest the development of a proposal which would have made it possible to enjoy all the charms of the area. Thus the architect Kisho Kurokawa, cofounder of the "Metabolism" Movement in the 1960's, proposed a form which would "spill over" into the countryside. This idea was reinforced by the use of a structure with curved lines and completely glazed façades, which would be protected from excessive sunlight by generous eaves and curtains designed to shift automatically with the movement of the sun.

Cette maison, non construite, devait s'établir en pente au bord de la mer, ce qui octroyait au projet une vue privilégiée. Ce magnifique emplacement semblait suggérer le développement d'un projet qui permettrait d'exploiter tous les charmes du lieu. C'est ainsi que l'architecte Kisho Kurokawa, co-fondateur du mouvement du "Métabolisme" dans les années 60, propose une planimétrie qui "déborde" sur le paysage. Cette impression est renforcée par l'utilisation d'une volumétrie de lignes courbes et de façades entièrement vitrées, protégées du soleil grâce à de grands auvents et rideaux qui se déplacent automatiquement avec celui-ci.

Dieses bislang nicht errichtete Haus war ursprünglich vorgesehen, an einer Steilküste am Meeresufer gebaut zu werden, was dem Projekt herrliche Aussichten gewährt. Dieser attraktive Standort beeinflußte die Entwicklung einer Planung für ein Projekt, von dem aus alle Vorzüge des Standortes ausgenutzt werden. Dementsprechend plant der Architekt Kisho Kurokawa, Mitbegründer der japanischen Architekturbewegung "Metabolismus" der 60er Jahre, eine Planimetrie, die in der Gegend "mündet". Diese Tatsache wird durch die Schaffung einer Volumetrie gekrümmter Linien und komplett verglaster Fassaden bestätigt, die von zu intensiver Sonnenbestrahlung durch großzügige Vordächer und Vorhänge geschützt werden, die sich automatisch je nach Position der Sonne bewegen.

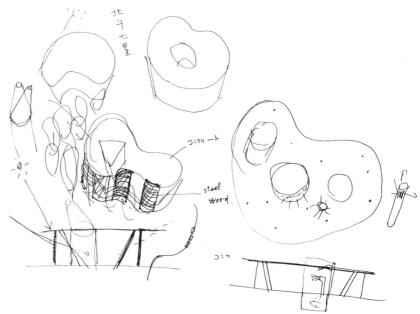

This project reflects the clear intention of enjoying the surroundings to the utmost, hence it is filled with references to the countryside through the use of shapes peering out over the land, either from the perimeter – the areas outside the house – or from within the structure – the terraces.

Ce projet reflète la nette intention de profiter le plus possible de l'environnement, mise à exécution à travers des formes qui se détachent au-dessus de la maison, aussi bien au niveau de la planimétrie – espaces extérieurs – que de la volumétrie – terrasses.

Durch dieses Projekt wird die klare Absicht deutlich, die Umgebung maximal genießen zu wollen. Somit wird also auf vielfältige Art an das Umfeld angeknüpft, durch Elemente, die ihm zugewandt sind. Dies wird sowohl in der Planimetrie deutlich, durch außerhalb des Hauses angeordnete Bereiche, als auch in der Volumetrie, durch Terrassen.

443

STAINLESS-STEEL HOUSE WITH LIGHT LATTICE

SHOEI YOH + ARCHITECTS

Nagasaki-shi, Japan. 1980

With this house, Shoei Yoh begins his investigations into the proposal of buildings as if they were environmental systems. He develops constructive and structural methods on the basis of the dialogue established with the surrounding countryside. The proposal for this house was based on a volume built "by" light by means of a latticework in criss-cross which forms the basis for the organization of the project: its structure, windows, ceilings and partition walls. Thin glazed bands were introduced between the panels in order to create ribbons of light in the interior during the day, while at night these transform the building into an attractive grid work projecting light towards the exterior.

À partir de ce projet, Shoei Yoh commence ses recherches sur la manière de concevoir des bâtiments comme s'ils faisaient partie de l'environnement. Il développe des méthodes où la construction et la structure s'élaborent à partir du dialogue qui s'établit avec la nature. Ce bâtiment est conçu à partir d'un volume "construit en lumière" grâce à un réticule orthogonal qui sert de base au projet : une structure principale avec fenêtres, plafonds et murs intérieurs. Une fine bande de verre s'introduit entre les jointures des panneaux, ce qui permet de laisser passer des rais de lumière dans la pièce pendant la journée, et de projeter de la lumière à l'extérieur la nuit à travers le superbe réticule.

Ausgehend von diesem Haus startet Shoei Yoh seine Forschungen auf dem Gebiet der Projektierung von Gebäuden, als wären es Umweltsysteme. Er entwickelte Bau- und Strukturmethoden, die ausgehend vom Dialog mit der Natur ausgearbeitet werden. Die Planung dieses Hauses basiert auf einem Baukörper, der "aus" Licht gebaut ist. Das Projekt besticht durch ein orthogonales Netz in der Struktur, den Fenstern, Überdachungen und Innenwänden. An den Verbindungspunkten der Paneele ist eine feine verglaste Bande eingefügt, die tagsüber Licht in den Innenraum einfallen lassen, während das Gebäude nachts zu einem stilvollen Netz wird, durch welches das Licht nach außen projiziert wird.

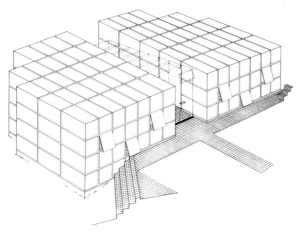

The floor plan of the house, measuring a total of 125 m²., is divided into three areas which are clearly differentiated: the space destined for public use is separated from the private area by an intermediate space filled with light.

Cette maison de 125 m² au total est divisée en trois zones nettement différenciées : la partie pour les invités, la zone privée, et la pièce intermédiaire qui les sépare, et qui concentre toute la lumière.

Die Gesamtoberfläche des Hauses von 125 m² ist in drei deutlich abgegrenzte Bereiche aufgeteilt. Der öffentlich zugängliche Bereich ist vom Privatbereich durch einen Zwischenraum aus Licht getrennt.

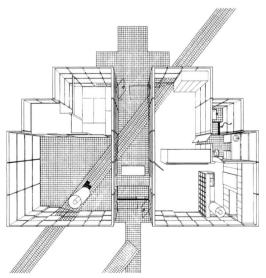

The fine glazed bands which join the panels break down the boundaries of the building which permits the entire house to be perceived as if it were made of light.

Les fines bandes de verre qui relient les panneaux entre eux divisent les limites du bâtiment ; ainsi toute la maison est perçue comme si elle était faite de lumière.

Die feinen Glasbande, die als Verbindung zwischen Paneelen dienen, zerlegen die Grenzen des Gebäudes, wodurch das komplette Haus wahrgenommen wird, als wäre es aus Licht gebaut.

STAINLESS-STEEL HOUSE WITH LIGHT LATTICE

SoMa house

Jim Jennings

San Franciso, USA. 2002

This was the project which initiated the reconversion process for the district of SoMa (South Market), a transition neighbourhood between an industrial zone and a commercial area where many of the residences were originally destined for non-residential uses. The program consisted of the transformation of a commercial building into a residence and studio. The main façade conserves an almost industrial character with *corten* steel as the predominant material. The spatial organization is composed of two areas separated by a courtyard which provides privacy to a guesthouse destined for occasional use in the smaller volume.

Ce projet marque le début du processus de reconversion de l'arrondissement de SoMa (South Market), un quartier de transition entre zone industrielle et commerciale, où une grande partie des habitations sont, à l'origine, des espaces destinés à d'autres fonctions. Le projet consiste à transformer un bâtiment à usage commercial en une résidence et un studio. La façade principale a su conserver un caractère quasi-industriel, utilisant comme matériel dominant l'acier corten. L'organisation spatiale est composée de deux pièces séparées par un bâtio, permettant de préserver l'intimité d'une éventuelle maison réservée aux invités dans le plus petit volume.

Mit diesem Projekt wird der Sanierungsprozess des Stadtteils SoMa (South Market) begonnen. Die Gegend bildet den Übergang vom Industriegebiet zur Einkaufszone, und viele sich dort befindenden Wohnhäuser wurden ursprünglich für andere Zwecke errichtet. Das Programm besteht aus der Umwandlung eines Gebäudes, das für kommerzielle Zwecke genutzt wurde, in ein Wohnhaus. Die Hauptfassade macht durch den hauptsächlichen Einsatz von Stahl einen fast industriellen Eindruck. Die räumliche Anordnung basiert auf zwei durch einen Innenhof voneinander getrennten Abschnitten. Dadurch wird die Privatsphäre in dem gelegentlich genutzten Gästehaus im kleineren Baukörper garantiert.

The floor plan is designed around two elements separated by a large courtyard. This division facilitates the separation of the different areas of the program.

Le plan est formé de deux éléments séparés par un patio. Cette division facilite la répartition des différentes fonctions de la maison.

Der Grundriss beruht auf zwei Elementen, die durch einen großen Innenhof voneinander getrennt sind. Dadurch wird auch die Aufteilung der Nutzung des Programmes erleichtert.

SOMA HOUSE

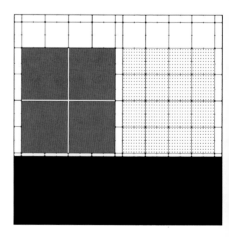

CASA TAGLE

LUIS IZQUIERDO, ANTONIA LEHMANN

Santiago de Chile, Chile. 1998-2000

\\ "The reason architecture strives to essentially go beyond mere construction is its aspiration for permanence" (L. Izquierdo). This need for permanence through the passing of time is related not only to the quality of the architecture, but also, in a more immediate aspect, to the type of materials used either due to their intrinsic properties or for the characteristics which they may bestow upon the architectural image. From this we can understand the importance of the investigations carried out by these designers for their work in the use of concrete. In this case, as in others, the use of concrete is the basic theme for many aspects of the project.

\\ "La raison qui fait que l'architecture va fondamentalement plus loin que la simple construction réside dans le désir de permanence" (L. Izquierdo). Ce besoin de permanence dans le temps est lié à la qualité de l'architecture, mais aussi, dans une optique plus immédiate, au type de matériel utilisé aussi bien pour ses propriétés intrinsèques que pour le caractère qu'il peut donner à l'image architecturale. D'où l'importance de la recherche réalisée par les auteurs de cette œuvre sur l'utilisation du béton. Dans ce bâtiment, comme dans beaucoup d'autres, le béton est le fil conducteur de nombreux aspects du projet.

\\ "Der Grund, warum die Architektur wesentlich die bloße Baukunst übertrifft, ist das Streben nach Beständigkeit." (L. Izquierdo). Dieses Streben nach zeitlicher Beständigkeit ist zum einen mit der Qualität der Architektur verbunden und zum anderen speziell mit der Art und Weise des Materialeinsatzes. Die Materialien spielen eine entscheidende Rolle, aufgrund ihrer eigenen Beschaffenheit und dem architektonischen Eindruck, den sie dem Gebäude verleihen können. Daher ist die Erforschung der Möglichkeiten bei der Verwendung von Beton, der von diesen Architekten in ihrem Werk eingesetzt wird, von großer Bedeutung. In diesem Haus, wie auch in anderen, ist der Beton der Leitfaden für viele Aspekte des Projektes.

CASA TAGLE

During development of the project, the handling of the openings in the concrete walls makes it possible to achieve an image of lightness in the structure in spite of the solidity of the material.

Pendant l'élaboration du projet, le traitement des ouvertures dans les plans de béton a permis de donner une image de légèreté malgré la solidité du matériel.

Bei der Entwicklung des Projektes wurden die Öffnungen in den Betonflächen so gestaltet, dass dem Baukörper trotz der Beständigkeit des Materials ein Bild der Leichtigkeit verliehen wird.

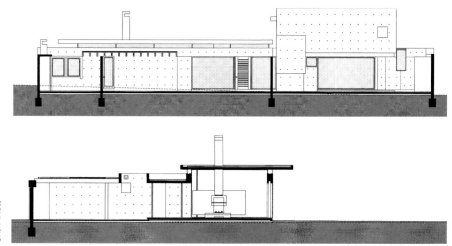

CASA TAGLE

The floor plan of this residence, located to the east of the city of Santiago, stretches out across the full width of the plot. The required regulations oblige it to be in alignment with the neighbouring houses.

Le plan de cette maison, située à l'est de la ville de Santiago, s'étend sur toute la largeur du terrain. Par respect des normes, son alignement est le même que pour les maisons voisines.

Dieses Wohnhaus, das östlich der Stadt Santiago errichtet wurde, erstreckt sich über die Länge des Grundstückes. Aufgrund der zu befolgenden Normen entspricht seine Anordnung derer der benachbarten Häuser.

CASA TAGLE

CASA TAGOMAGO

CARLOS FERRATER-JOAN GUIBERNAU

Ibiza, España. 1999 / 2001

A group of small, isolated pavilions dependent upon a main nucleus is one of the bases of the volumetric and spatial organization of this house, situated in Santa Eulalia del Rio, upon a lot with views over the sea and the island of Tagomago. In this manner, one of the constructive traditions of the region where these houses are built is respected, consisting of the addition of rooms and spaces around a main house. Some of the functional needs, however, are also provided for in this way: the intended holiday use of the residence implies both a spatial flexibility and flexibility in the number of inhabitants. Marés stone, white concrete and wood complete the image of this new Ibizan home.

Un noyau principal dont dépendent de petits pavillons isolés constitue l'une des bases de l'organisation volumétrique et spatiale de cette maison, située à Santa Eulalia del Río, sur un terrain avec vue sur la mer et sur l'île de Tagomago. Elle respecte ainsi les traditions de la région, où les maisons se construisent en ajoutant des pièces et des espaces autour d'un bâtiment principal, et parvient en même temps à répondre aux besoins fonctionnels. Utilisée pour les vacances, elle doit être flexible par rapport à l'espace et au nombre d'habitants. Les pierres, le béton blanc et le bois viennent compléter l'image de cette nouvelle maison à Ibiza.

Ein zentrales Gebäude, um das herum kleine abgelegene Pavillons angeordnet sind, ist eine der Grundlagen für die volumetrische und räumliche Anordnung dieses Hauses in Santa Eulalia del Río, auf einem Grundstück mit Blick auf das Meer und auf die Insel Tagomago. Somit wird eine der traditionellen Bauweisen der Gegend berücksichtigt, nach der die Häuser durch das Angliedern von Abschnitten und Räumen um das Haupthaus herum gebaut wurden. Jedoch werden somit auch die funktionellen Bedürfnisse gedeckt. Da das Projekt als Ferienhaus genutzt wird, ist die räumliche Anordnung flexibel und lässt eine variierende Anzahl an Bewohnern zu. Durch Meeresteine, weißen Beton und Holz wird das Design dieses neuen ibizenkischen Hauses vervollständigt.

CASA TAGOMAGO

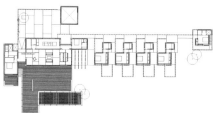

The design of exterior spaces devoid of gardens and the use of materials in their natural state endow the ensemble with an introverted character.

Le traitement de l'extérieur sans aménagement d'espaces verts et l'utilisation de matériel à l'état naturel donne à l'ensemble un caractère de recueillement.

Die Gestaltung der äußeren Bereiche ohne Begrünung und die Anwendung von Materialien in ihrem natürlichen Zustand geben dem Gesamtwerk eine Nuance der inneren Sammlung.

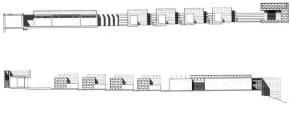

The constructive system matches the few materials used: stone walls, floors with concrete beams and ceramic vaults. The interior flooring is polished off with stone while that of the exterior, like the carpentry work, is wooden.

Le système constructif est en accord avec les matériaux utilisés, peu nombreux : murs de pierre, hourdis avec poutres en béton et voûtes en céramique. Dans la maison, le plancher est fini en pierre, et le revêtement extérieur tout comme les charpentes sont constitués de bois.

Das Bausystem entspricht der geringen Anzahl an verwendeten Materialien, wie Mauern aus Stein, gestützt durch Betonträger und Keramikgewölbe. Die Innenbereiche wurden mit Stein gepflastert, während die Außenbereiche mit Holz verkleidet sind.

CASA TAGOMAGO

TAKAHATA HOUSE

ATELIER KO + MALO PLANNING

Yamagata, Japan. 2000-2002

This house situated in the north of Japan in a region of hard winters, is currently the only one in existence in this new residential project. Nonetheless, the prevision for the construction of neighbouring buildings made it necessary to propose a plan which would maintain the privacy of this residence even when the surroundings are fully built over. Thus the house establishes its own "neighbours" spatially: as in a house with a courtyard, a series of perimeter bedrooms surrounds a central double height living-room. Structurally, this space is reflected by a bi-level roof which, on the other hand, facilitates the optimum functioning of the house during the tough winter snowstorms.

Cette maison qui se trouve au nord du Japon, dans une zone à l'hiver rude, est actuellement la seule de ce nouveau complexe résidentiel. Cependant, le projet de construction de maisons voisines a obligé à prévoir une structure pouvant préserver l'intimité de la maison une fois celle-ci entourée d'autres bâtiments. Cette maison introduit spatialement ses propres "voisins" : à la manière d'une maison-patio, une série de chambres entourent un salon central à double hauteur. D'une perspective volumétrique, cet espace se reflète au travers d'une toiture à deux niveaux qui favorise le bon fonctionnement de la maison pendant les fortes chutes de neige hivernales.

Dieses Haus im Norden Japans, in einem Gebiet mit sehr kalten Wintern, ist zur Zeit das einzige Gebäude, das im Rahmen dieser neuen Wohnraumerschließung errichtet wurde. Da jedoch der Bau weiterer Gebäude vorgesehen ist, sollte eine Planung entwickelt werden, die die Privatsphäre des Wohnhauses gewährleistet, obwohl sein Umfeld noch nicht bebaut ist. Somit werden also bei der räumlichen Gestaltung die "Nachbarn" einbezogen. Wie ein Innenhof wird das zentral angeordnete Wohnzimmer auf zwei Höhen von Räumen umgeben. Die Volumetrie beeindruckt durch ein auf zwei Höhen angeordnetes Dach, wodurch das Haus den starken Schneefällen im Winter optimal standhält.

TAKAHATA HOUSE

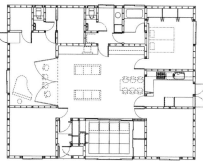

A music room is designed with direct access to the central area. Occasionally, these two areas may be joined together to form a small concert hall.

Une salle de musique est directement reliée à la pièce centrale. Ces deux espaces peuvent éventuellement se rejoindre pour former une petite salle de concerts.

Ein Musiksaal wird in direktem Bezug zum zentralen Bereich entworfen. Diese zwei Bereiche können schließlich vereint werden und somit einen kleinen Konzertsaal bilden.

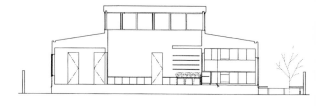

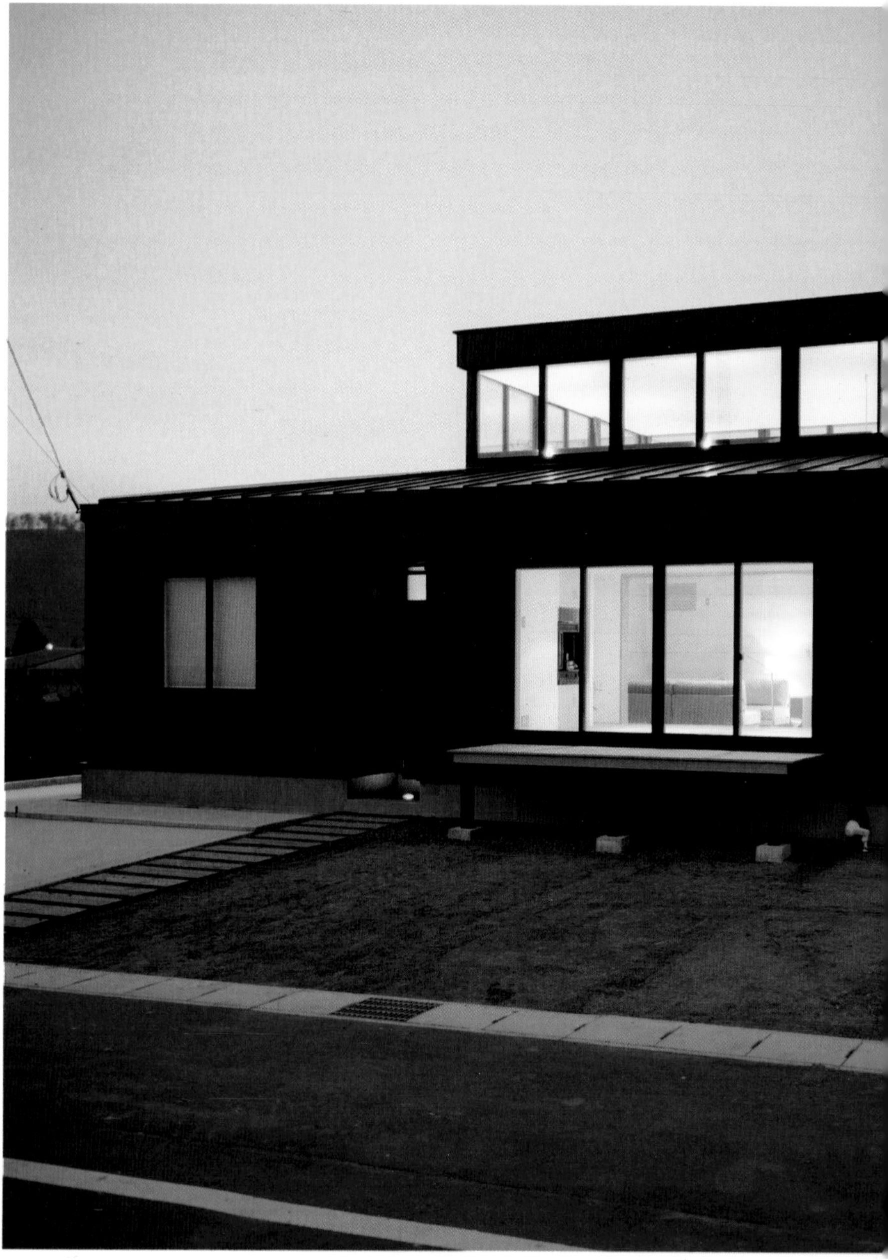

A flat rooftop keeps the snow piled up at the highest point of the structure. Thus it would only need to be cleared once or twice during the entire winter. Underneath, a second roof prevents accidents during the clearing process.

Le toit plat permet d'accumuler la neige sur le plus haut point du bâtiment, et ne doit donc être nettoyé qu'une ou deux fois pendant tout l'hiver. En dessous, un deuxième toit évite les incidents pendant ce procédé.

Durch ein flaches Dach wird der Schnee auf der höchsten Ebene des Baukörpers gesammelt. Somit muss es den gesamten Winter hindurch nur ein oder zweimal gesäubert werden. Durch ein zweites unterhalb angeordnetes Dach werden während der Säuberung Unfälle vermieden.

TAKAHATA HOUSE

WOHNHAUS TAUCHER

ERNST GISELBRECHT ARCHITEKT

Graz, Österreich. 1993-1995 / 1996

The proposal for this wooden house was based on a simple orthogonal design which starts off with the idea of a "box" with an opening in one corner. This situation is reflected both on the floor plan as well as on the façade. The solidity of the volume is reinforced by the introduction of small, controlled openings on the surface of the wood, while the effect of dissolution observed in the corner is emphasized by the use of glazed walls providing a total and complete transparency to the vertex of the box. As a crowning element, the rooftop redefines the characteristics of the volume.

Le concept de cette maison de pierre est un simple schéma orthogonal, qui part d'un "caisson" qui s'ouvre sur son angle. Cette situation est reflétée tant sur la vue en plan que sur la façade. L'aspect solide du volume est renforcé par l'introduction de petites embrasures contrôlées sur la surface de bois. A l'inverse, la dissolution produite au niveau de l'angle est accentuée par l'utilisation de surfaces vitrées qui permettent une transparence totale dans ce sommet du volume. Le plan du toit, élément final de l'œuvre, donne une nouvelle définition aux caractéristiques de la structure.

Die Planung dieses aus Holz errichteten Hauses basiert auf einer einfachen orthogonalen Anordnung, die von einem rechtwinkligen Baukörper ausgeht, der sich an einem Eckpunkt öffnet. Dies wird sowohl im Grund- als auch im Aufriss deutlich. Die Beständigkeit des Baukörpers wird durch die Anordnung kleiner und kontrollierter Öffnungen in der Oberfläche des Holzes verstärkt, während die Auflösung an einem der Eckpunkte durch den Einsatz von Glasflächen gesteigert wird, durch die an dieser Stelle eine vollkommene Transparenz geschaffen wird. Als abschließendes Element bestimmt der Grundriss des Daches die Eigenschaften des Baukörpers.

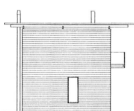

The volume of the terrace forms the contrasting element on the façade. Its red tones and horizontal lines break up the verticality of the main box.

Le volume de la terrasse sert d'élément de contraste avec la façade. De couleur rouge et aux proportions horizontales, il vient interrompre la verticalité du volume principal.

Die Terrasse wird zu einem Kontrastelement zur Fassade. Durch ihre rote Farbe und die horizontalen Proportionen entsteht ein Bruch mit der vertikalen Anordnung des Hauptbaukörpers.

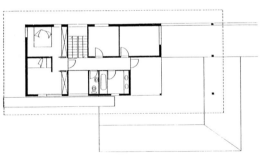

TEICH RESIDENCE

MURDOCK YOUNG ARCHITECTS

New Jersey, USA. 2002

Housing concepts have changed considerably since this dwelling was built in 1949. Originally designed for a family with domestic staff, many of its spaces were disconnected from the areas of scenic beauty and the views over the Manhattan skyline. In order to bring this project closer to modern housing concepts, the project was initiated with the idea of "opening" the house, both on the inside –by joining the compartmentalized spaces into one– and on the outside, by widening windows and creating spaces with direct communication to the exterior. Formally, thanks to the materials proposed, the project has acquired a completely updated image.

Le concept d'une maison a bien changé depuis la construction de cette habitation en 1949. Initialement conçue pour une famille employant du personnel de service, un grand nombre de ses pièces étaient coupées des attraits du lieu et des vues sur la ligne d'horizon de Manhattan. Afin d'adapter ce projet aux concepts actuels, on a commencé par "ouvrir" la maison, à l'intérieur – en transformant des pièces cloisonnées en une seule – comme à l'extérieur, en élargissant les fenêtres et en créant des espaces donnant directement sur l'extérieur. Au niveau des formes, et grâce aux matériaux utilisés, le projet a pu acquérir une image moderne.

Das Konzept über Wohnhäuser hat sich seit dem Bau dieses Hauses im Jahre 1949 beachtlich geändert. Es wurde ursprünglich für eine Familie mit Dienstpersonal entworfen, wodurch viele Bereiche von den Vorzügen des Standortes abgegrenzt waren und die Aussicht über die Skyline von Manhattan nicht möglich war. Um dieses Projekt entsprechend der heutigen Vorstellungen über Wohnhäuser zu gestalten, sollte das Haus in erster Linie "geöffnet" werden, sowohl nach innen, indem die getrennten Bereiche zu einem einzigen zusammengeführt werden, als auch nach außen, indem die Fenster vergrößert und direkt mit der äußeren Umgebung verbundene Bereiche geschaffen werden. Durch die formelle Gestaltung und den Einsatz der Materialien wird dem Projekt ein gänzlich moderner Eindruck verliehen.

The existing partition walls were eliminated from many of the interior spaces, converting them thus into spacious, attractive rooms dedicated to a variety of uses, for example the old kitchen which is now connected to a central nucleus.

De nombreuses séparations intérieures ont été éliminées pour en faire de grandes et magnifiques pièces à usage varié, comme par exemple l'ancienne cuisine, qui fonctionne désormais à partir d'un noyau central.

In einem Großteil der Innenräume wurden die räumlichen Abgrenzungen entfernt, um großräumige und stilvolle Bereiche zu schaffen, die auf unterschiedliche Weise genutzt werden können, wie zum Beispiel die ursprüngliche Küche, die heute ausgehend von einem zentralen Abschnitt genutzt wird.

TEICH RESIDENCE

The original windows became broad expanses of glass which take full advantage of the exterior and its views.

Les fenêtres d'origine ont été agrandies pour se convertir en de grands vitrages qui permettent d'exploiter au maximum l'extérieur et les différents angles de vision.

Die Originalfenster wurden zu großen Glasflächen erweitert, wodurch die äußere Umgebung und die Aussichten maximal genossen werden können.

THOMAS RESIDENCE

MACK ARCHITECTS

Las Vegas, USA. 1997

One of the virtues of the work of this Californian architect is the way in which his buildings relate to the surroundings. As a result, his projects make reference to their location using the formal and constructive tradition. This house was designed from the inside outwards in accordance with his ideas and respecting the local restrictions. Thus, a central nucleus formed by a courtyard is the starting point, from which the spaces are organized "outwards". As the design moves away from the centre, the house begins to dematerialize into successive layers of walls which stretch out over the area. In this manner an attractive network of relationships is produced between the house and its surroundings.

L'un des avantages de l'œuvre de cet architecte californien est la manière dont ses bâtiments se rattachent au milieu environnant. Dès lors, ses projets font référence au lieu au moyen d'une tradition des formes et de la construction. En accord avec ses idées, et en respect des restrictions imposées, cette maison se développe depuis l'intérieur vers l'extérieur. Ainsi, un noyau central se détache, formé par un patio, à partir duquel s'organisent les espaces "vers l'extérieur". Plus on s'éloigne du centre, plus la maison se dématérialise à travers une série de murs qui s'étendent tout autour de celle-ci. De cette manière, on se trouve face à un intéressant tissage qui relie la maison à son environnement.

Einer der Vorzüge des Werkes dieses Architekten aus Kalifornien liegt in der Art und Weise, wie sie mit dem Standort in Bezug gesetzt werden. Aus diesem Grund wird die traditionelle formelle Anordnung und Bauweise genutzt, um die Projekte auf den Standort zu beziehen. Seiner Sichtweise entsprechend und gemäß der Einschränkungen des Standortes wurde dieses Haus von innen nach außen geschaffen. Somit wird von einem zentralen Punkt ausgegangen, der durch einen Innenhof gebildet wird und von dem aus die Bereiche "nach außen" entstehen. Ausgehend vom Zentrum des Hauses löst sich die Baustruktur nach außen hin immer weiter in vereinzelte Mauern auf. Somit entstehen auf stilvolle Weise verflochtene Beziehungen des Hauses zu seiner Umgebung.

The use of colour on the walls is of great importance for the relationships with the surroundings. The colours chosen allow the walls to be perceived as a backdrop to the area.

L'emploi de couleur sur les murs est très important par rapport aux relations avec l'environnement. Les couleurs utilisées permettent une interprétation des plans comme la toile de fond du paysage.

Die farbliche Gestaltung der Mauern ist für die Beziehung zur Umgebung von großer Bedeutung. Durch die verwendeten Farben wirken die Flächen wie Hintergründe der Gegend.

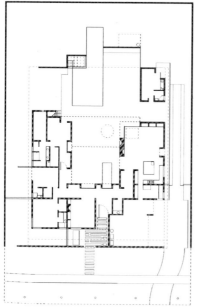

CASA TÍ Y CIÓ

ENRIC MASSIP BOSCH, ARQUITECTO

Tarragona, España. 1993-1995

One of the starting points of this project, located in Falset on the outskirts of Tarragona, was to occupy only a portion of the terrain leaving the greater part of the land free. This decision was also due in part to the need to comply with local regulations. A volume with straight lines and a narrow ground plan is organized over different floors in order to complete the program. Formally the volume is perceived as unique, although as the needs –both interior and exterior– vary, different elements emerge from it creating an interesting play of light and shadow upon a form which was originally flat.

'un des points de départ de ce projet situé à Falset, à la périphérie de Tarragone, était d'occuper seulement une partie du terrain pour laisser le plus d'espace libre possible. Cette décision permettait aussi de respecter la réglementation imposée. Un volume de lignes droites et de dimensions étroites se développe à différents niveaux pour mettre à bien le projet. Du point de vue des formes, le volume est perçu comme un ensemble unique, mais par rapport aux besoins intérieurs et extérieurs, des éléments s'en détachent, ce qui donne un intéressant jeu d'ombres et de lumières à une géométrie initialement plane.

Einer der Ausgangspunkte im Rahmen dieses Projektes, das sich in Falset am Rande der Provinz Tarragona befindet, war, nur einen Abschnitt des Geländes zu bebauen und soviel Freiraum wie möglich zu erhalten. Diese Entscheidung wurde unter anderem den Normen des Standortes entsprechend getroffen. Gemäß der Planung wurde ein Baukörper mit geraden Linien und schmalen Ausmaßen entworfen. Formell wird der Baukörper als Einheit wahrgenommen, obwohl sowohl in den Außenbereichen als auch den Innenräumen Elemente hervortreten, die auf der ursprünglich flächigen Geometrie einen angenehmen Licht-Schatten-Effekt erzeugen.

The construction method used, as well as the insulation system proposed, is extended throughout the construction of the entire house. The roof with the same constructive criteria, becomes what the designer calls "the upper façade".

La méthode utilisée pour la construction ainsi que le système d'isolation s'étendent à toute la maison. Le toit, qui respecte les mêmes critères de construction, se transforme en ce que l'auteur appelle "façade supérieure".

Die angewandte Bauweise und das eingefügte Isoliersystem bestimmen die Konstruktion des gesamten Hauses. Das Dach, das ebenfalls den Kriterien dieser Bauweise entspricht, wird zu dem, was der Architekt als "obere Fassade" bezeichnet.

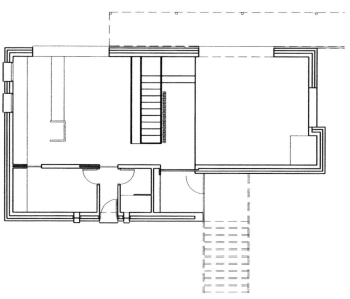

VIESEL HOUSE

AUGUSTIN UND FRANK ARCHITEKTEN

Falkensee, Deutschland. 1999

One of the requirements of the owners –a pair of booksellers– was that the house be capable of holding 370 metres of books. Starting from this important necessity, the designers proposed an architectural plan based on the needs of the program, thus developing a project spread out over two floors. The upper floor was to hold the main bulk of the books while the task of the lower floor was, literally, to support the weight of these books. As a result of this partition, two elements were assigned to the volume, each in accordance with its specific function: a solid concrete piece on the lower floor provides the base for a light wooden structure which rests upon it.

A la requête des propriétaires, un couple de libraires, cette maison devait accueillir 370 mètres de livres. A partir de cet important critère, les auteurs ont proposé une architecture basée sur les besoins du projet. Cette maison à deux niveaux contient la majorité des livres à l'étage, tandis que le rez-de-chaussée sert à supporter leur poids. En conséquence de cette bipartition, et en accord avec ses fonctions, deux éléments donnent forme au volume : une solide pièce de béton au niveau bas qui sert de soubassement à une structure légère de bois, laquelle s'appuie sur cet élément.

Im Rahmen des Auftrages der Eigentümer, die im Buchhandel tätig sind, sollen im Haus Bücherregale auf einer Länge von 370 Metern Platz haben. Ausgehend von diesem wichtigen Kriterium wird die Architektur entsprechend dieser Bedürfnisse geplant. Somit wird ein zweistöckiges Projekt entwickelt, dessen obere Etage für die Mehrheit der Bücher konzipiert ist, während die untere Etage buchstäblich dem Gewicht standhalten soll. Durch diese Zweiteilung besteht der Baukörper aus zwei Elementen, die gemäß ihrer Funktionen angeordnet sind. Ein beständiges Element aus Beton im Erdgeschoss dient als Fundament für eine leichte Struktur aus Holz, die darauf gestützt ist.

This house, located in the suburbs of Berlin, represents an example of the changes in one family's lifestyle. Many of the inhabitants of the city are moving to the suburbs in order to forge stronger relations with nature while still remaining close to the city.

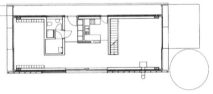

Cette maison, qui se trouve aux alentours de Berlin, constitue un exemple du changement dans les habitudes de vie d'une famille. De nombreux habitants de cette ville ont déménagé à l'extérieur pour un meilleur contact avec la nature tout en restant près de la ville.

Dieses Haus am Stadtrand von Berlin ist ein Beispiel für die Änderung der familiären Lebensgewohnheiten. Viele Einwohner der Großstadt ziehen in die Vororte, um der Natur näher zu sein und trotzdem in der Nähe der Stadt zu wohnen.

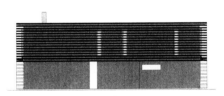

VIESEL HOUSE

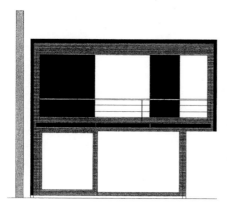

An envelope of horizontal planes protects the house from neighbouring buildings. This membrane generates greater respect within the project towards the surroundings, in addition to projecting a pleasing light into the interior.

Un ensemble de plans horizontaux protège la maison des bâtiments voisins. Cette membrane, en plus de projeter une agréable lumière à l'intérieur, instaure une relation de respect par rapport au paysage environnant.

Das Haus wird durch eine Schicht horizontal angeordneter Streben von den umliegenden Häusern abgegrenzt. Durch diese Art der Abgrenzung kann in die Innenräume ein angenehmes Licht einfallen und der Respekt des Projektes dem Umfeld gegenüber bewahrt werden.

VOS HOUSE

KOEN VAN VELSEN

Amsterdam, The Netherlands. 1999

This single family dwelling on the island of Borneo reflects a refined study of the project and its needs. Due to its position between party walls, it only presents two façades: one towards the street and the other facing the canal. Thus a concrete "skin" folds itself up following a continuous rhythm of rectangular openings, until it bcomes transformed into both a façade and a roof. In this manner a foreground forming both the façade and roof was proposed, "concealing" a second, glazed skin beneath it. This allowed the interior spaces to be organized to a more casual rhythm around a great triple height courtyard.

Cette maison individuelle, située sur l'île de Bornéo, reflète l'étude soignée du projet et de ses besoins. Dû aux caractéristiques du terrain, avec deux côtés libres seulement, cette habitation ne présente que deux façades : une vers la rue et l'autre vers le canal. Ainsi, une enveloppe extérieure de béton au rythme continu d'ouvertures rectangulaires se plie pour former à la fois une façade et un toit. Ce premier plan de façade et de toit "dissimule" une seconde enveloppe vitrée qui permet l'organisation des espaces intérieurs avec un rythme plus libre autour d'un grand patio à triple hauteur.

Dieses Einfamilienhaus auf der Insel Borneo basiert auf einer ausgefeilten Studie des Projektes und seinen Ansprüchen. Aufgrund seiner Lage verfügt das Wohnhaus nur über zwei Fassaden, die jeweils zur Straße und zum Kanal hin ausgerichtet sind. Durch eine Schicht aus Beton, die fortlaufend und regelmäßig durch rechteckige Öffnungen unterbrochen wird, zeichnet sich sowohl die Fassade als auch das Dach aus. Durch diese Planung sind also zunächst die Fassade und das Dach aus Beton zu sehen, durch die wie eine zweite Haut eine verglaste Schicht "versteckt" wird, wodurch die Innenräume freier angeordnet werden können und sogar ein großer Innenhof Platz hat.

VOS HOUSE

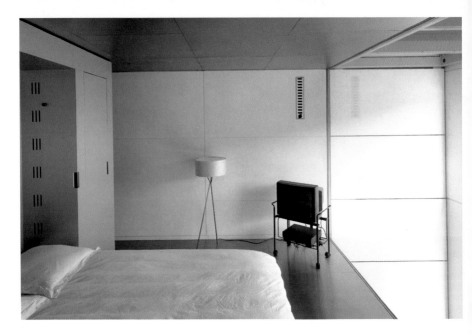

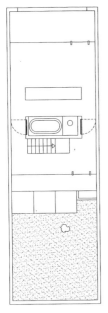

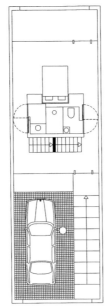

The residence with an area of 140 m². was developed over 4 floors containing a studio, bedroom, kitchen-dining-room and living-room respectively. As in the case of the exterior, strict control in the use of the materials was maintained in the interior.

Ce bâtiment de 140m² se développe sur quatre étages qui contiennent le studio, la chambre, la cuisine-salle à manger et la salle principale respectivement. Dès lors, un contrôle strict des matériaux utilisés est observé, dedans comme dehors.

Das Wohnhaus mit einer Gesamtoberfläche von 140m² ist in vier Bereiche eingeteilt, ein Büro, ein Zimmer, die Küche und das Wohn- und Esszimmer. Wie auch in den Außenbereichen wird der Einsatz der Materialien in den Innenräumen streng kontrolliert.

VOS HOUSE

WEEKEND HOUSE

OFFICE OF RYUE NISHIZAWA. RYUE NISHIZAWA, KIMIHIKO OKADA

Usui-gun, Gunma Prefecture, Japan. 1997 / 1998

The formal austerity present in the work of Ryue Nishizawa is the result of the study of the conditions affecting the project, rather than a stylistic choice *a priori*. In this house located 2 hours away from Tokyo, the proposal is the result of the analysis of the characteristics of the commission –including the need for an art exhibition area– as well as of the local conditions – an almost completely uninhabited woodland. As a result (and for security reasons) the house is closed off towards the exterior organized around 3 interior/inner courtyards. The diaphanous space is thus compartmentalized by the introduction of these 3 elements, which provide light and ventilation to the house.

L'austérité des formes dans l'œuvre de Ryue Nishizawa est davantage le résultat de l'étude des caractéristiques du projet qu'un choix stylistique a priori. *Dans cette maison, qui se trouve à deux heures de Tokyo, le plan est le fruit de l'analyse des particularités de la commande, ici le besoin d'une salle pour les expositions, et des caractéristiques environnantes – une zone boisée pratiquement deserte. Par conséquent (et par sécurité), la maison se ferme à l'extérieur et s'organise autour de trois patios intérieurs. Ainsi, l'espace diaphane se divise pour introduire ces trois éléments, qui apportent air et lumière à la maison.*

Die formelle Strenge des Werkes von Ryue Nishizawa ist nicht in erster Linie durch stilistisches Empfinden entstanden. Es ist vielmehr das Ergebnis einer Studie über die Bedingungen des Projektes. Die Planung dieses zwei Stunden von Tokio entfernten Hauses ist das Ergebnis einer Analyse der Inhalte des Auftrages, demzufolge ein Ausstellungsraum benötigt wird. Weiterhin hängt die Planung von den Bedingungen des Standortes ab, der bewaldet und fast unbewohnt ist. Daher (und auch aus Sicherheitsgründen) wird das Haus nach außen hin verschlossen und erhält stattdessen drei Innenhöfe. Auf diese Weise wird der offene Bereich durch diese drei Elemente aufgeteilt, durch die das Haus beleuchtet und belüftet wird.

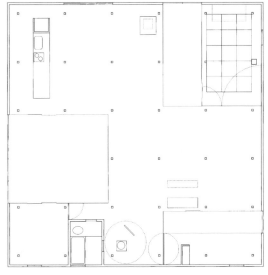

A 2,4 m. gridwork forms the basis of the floor plan. The spatial variety in the proposal belies its simplicity. Thus the introduction of three courtyards differentiates the distinct parts of the house.

Un réticule de 2,4 m sert de base à l'organisation de l'étage. Malgré la simplicité du projet, la diversité spatiale n'a pas été négligée. L'introduction de trois patios permet de différencier les diverses fonctions de la maison.

Der Entwurf des Grundrisses basiert auf einer gleichmäßigen Anordnung von 2,4 m² großen Abschnitten. Durch die Klarheit der Planung wird jedoch trotzdem die räumliche Vielfalt bewahrt. Somit wird durch die Anordnung dreier Innenhöfe die Verteilung der verschiedenen Nutzungsbereiche des Hauses ermöglicht.

WOHNHAUS WEGMAN

BEHNISCH & PARTNER. MANFRED SABATKE

Ingolstadt, Deutschland. 1997-1998

This German architect and his team cannot really be "classified" under any particular style. Their approaches are based more on the need to achieve solutions which investigate within the specific nature of each commission, rather than on the search for innovation. Hence it is not surprising that their projects should be so disparate. In the case of the residential sector they provide few examples. Even so a limited number of connections can be found between these examples, although they received the commission for this house thanks to the "Haus Charlotte" (1993). What both solutions have in common is the choice of materials and the use of ecological principles.

Il n'y a pas de style particulier dans lequel on peut "classifier" cet architecte allemand et son équipe. La mise en œuvre de leurs projets est davantage basée sur le besoin de trouver des solutions qui correspondent à chaque commande spécifique que sur la quête de l'innovation. Il n'est donc pas étonnant de voir des œuvres si différentes les unes des autres. Les exemples sont peu nombreux dans le cas de la typologie résidentielle. Toutefois, ils ont pu grâce à la "Haus Charlotte" (1993) être chargés de la commande de la présente maison. Ces deux édifices ont en commun les matériaux utilisés et le recours à des principes écologiques.

Es gibt keinen eindeutigen Stil, dem dieser deutsche Architekt und sein Team zugeordnet werden können. Die Ansätze basieren nicht so sehr auf der Suche nach Innovation, sondern eher auf der Notwendigkeit, Lösungen zu finden, die sich in der Individualität jedes Auftrages verstecken. Daher überrascht es nicht, dass sich ihre Projekte so sehr voneinander unterscheiden. Obwohl sie auf dem Gebiet der Wohnhäuser nur wenige Exemplare zu bieten haben, zwischen denen nur begrenzte Zusammenhänge bestehen, wurden sie durch das "Haus Charlotte" (1993) mit diesem Projekt beauftragt. In beiden Projekten kamen dieselben Materialien dasselbe ökologische Prinzip zum Einsatz.

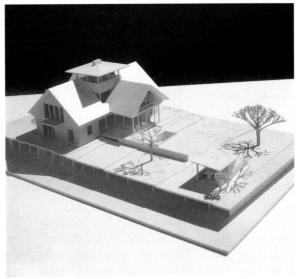

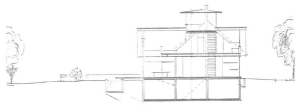

529

This house is an example of its creator's design process. The client, who upon beholding the Charlotte House desired a similar type of roof, happened to own a lot with very diverse characteristics. For this reason the result is also quite distinct.

Cette maison est l'exemple du processus de conception de l'auteur. Après avoir vu la maison Charlotte, le client voulait un toit similaire. Le résultat obtenu sur ce terrain aux caractéristiques très variées est différent.

Dieses Haus ist ein Beispiel dafür, wie das Design vom Architekten gestaltet wird. Der Auftraggeber verlangte ein Dach, das dem des Hauses Charlotte ähnelte. Da er jedoch über ein Grundstück mit einer ganz anderen Beschaffenheit verfügte, gelangte man auch zu einem anderen Resultat.

WOHNHAUS WEGMAN

In the intersection of the gabled roofs, an attractive viewpoint, which has become one of the most privileged areas of the house, has been designed.

A l'intersection des toitures à deux versants se projette un superbe mirador, l'un des espaces les plus privilégiés de la maison.

Am Winkel des Giebeldaches ein stilvoller Aussichtsbereich errichtet, der somit zu einem der schönsten Räume des Hauses wird.

WOHNHAUS WIERICH

DÖRING, DAHMEN, JOERESSEN ARCHITEKTEN

Recklinghausen, Deutschland. 1995

In many of the works of this German team, we find the use of pure structural volumes or structures which are developed out of variations governed by geometric norms of great clarity. In this house, a single volume developed along the formal guidelines of a cube contains the functional areas of the home. A second element evolving out of this volume is a wall rotating out of the façade at a 45° angle; this opens the house out towards the garden. The directions suggested by this angle lead towards a gallery which enriches the open spaces of the dwelling. Finally, a small summerhouse completes the development of the ensemble.

On trouve dans beaucoup des oeuvres de cette équipe allemande l'utilisation de volumétries pures ou développées à partir de variations déterminées par des règles géométriques très claires. Dans cette maison, un volume unique basé sur des formes cubiques contient les espaces nobles de la maison. De ce volume se détache un second élément qui se développe à partir d'un plan en rotation de 45° de la première façade et ouvre la maison sur le jardin. Les directions empruntées par cette inclinaison mènent à une galerie qui enrichit l'espace ouvert de l'habitation. Un petit pavillon se joint à l'ensemble pour le compléter.

In vielen Werken dieses deutschen Teams kommen klare Volumetrien zum Ausdruck, die durch geometrische Normen von großer Klarheit variiert werden. Dieses Haus besteht aus einem einzigen Baukörper mit der formellen Struktur eines Würfels, in dem die stilvollen Bereiche des Hauses angeordnet sind. Von diesem Baukörper ausgehend wird in einem Winkel von 45° zu seiner Fassade ein zweites Element geschaffen, wodurch das Haus zum Garten hin geöffnet wird. Die durch diesen Winkel entstehende Ausrichtung führt zu einer Galerie, durch die der offene Bereich des Wohnhauses bereichert wird. Das Gesamtwerk wird schließlich durch einen kleinen Pavillon vervollständigt.

A rectangle marks off the general boundaries of the house. On one side an opening towards the exterior is produced through the introduction of a triangle which rotates 45° out of the rectangular façade.

Un rectangle délimite l'enceinte de la maison. Un triangle en rotation de 45° à partir de la façade rectangulaire permet une ouverture latérale vers l'extérieur.

Der allgemeine Bereich des Hauses ist rechteckig, und auf einer Seite ist er nach außen hin geöffnet, durch ein Dreieck, das in einem Winkel von 45° zur Fassade des Rechteckes angeordnet ist.

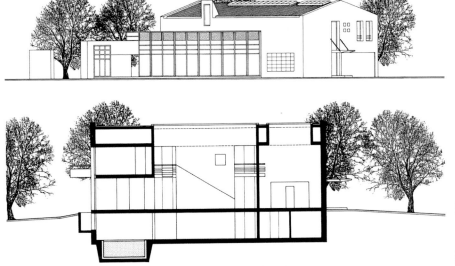

WOHNHAUS WIERICH

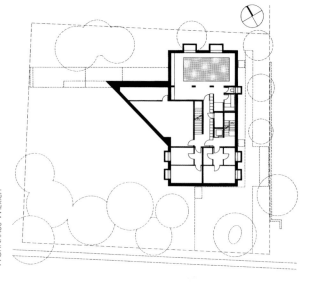

In addition to the main residence, the building also includes an apartment on the upper floor, which is entered by a separate staircase which can nevertheless be connected to the main house.

Ce bâtiment, en plus de l'habitation principale, contient un appartement à l'étage, auquel on accède par un escalier séparé qui peut toutefois se rattacher à la maison.

Das Gesamtwerk besteht in erster Linie aus einer Wohnung. Im Obergeschoss befindet sich weiterhin ein Apartment, zu dem der Zugang über eine eigene Treppe ermöglicht wird, die jedoch auch an die Treppe des Haupthauses angeschlossen werden kann.

Y.S House

Itsuko Hasegawa

Tokyo, Japan. 2000-2001

Y.s. House is located in a building which also holds a pharmacy and 3 clinics, leaving the upper floor free for the residence. This situation created great virtues such as the panoramic views over the city skyline; it was also exploited to produce a contrast between the occupational uses of the different floors: while on the lower floors all of the available area is used, on the upper floor terraces were created for the enjoyment of the views. In the formal solution, all the partitions are made of glazed blue blocks which lend an attractive image to the structure, that of an element floating over the city.

La maison Y.S occupe le dernier étage d'un ensemble qui contient également une pharmacie et trois cliniques. Cet emplacement comporte de nombreux avantages, comme par exemple une vue panoramique sur la ligne d'horizon de la ville. En outre, il crée un intéressant contraste quant à l'emploi des différents étages : alors qu'aux niveaux inférieurs, tout l'espace disponible est utilisé, la présence de terrasses au dernier étage permet d'admirer la vue. Vis-à-vis des formes, tous les bardages sont réalisés à partir d'un bloc de verre bleuté, ce qui donne au bâtiment la majestueuse image d'un élément flottant au-dessus de la ville.

Die im Obergeschoss liegende Wohnung ist Bestandteil des Gesamtprojekts Y.S, zu dem auch eine Apotheke und drei Kliniken gehören. Durch den Standort werden dem Gebäude große Vorzüge verliehen, wie zum Beispiel die herrlichen Aussichten über die Skyline der Stadt. Diese Lage wird jedoch auch genutzt, um einen Kontrast in der Nutzung der verschiedenen Etagen zu schaffen. Während in den unteren Etagen die zur Verfügung stehenden Räumlichkeiten vollkommen ausgenutzt werden, befinden sich im Obergeschoss Terrassen, von denen aus man die Aussichten genießen kann. Was die formelle Gestaltung betrifft, wurden die Fassaden des Gebäudes mit einer blauen Verglasung ausgestattet, wodurch dem Baukörper einen stilvollen Eindruck vermittelt, als würde er über der Stadt schweben.

Y.S House

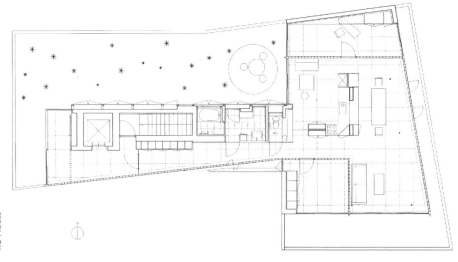

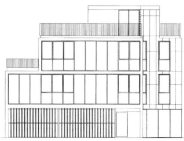

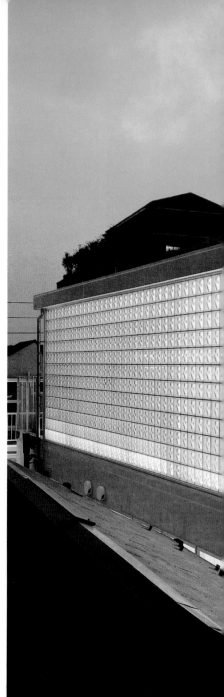

The decision to convert this residence into an attic allows its inhabitants to enjoy the skyline of the city of Tokyo, far removed from its real chaos.

La décision d'établir ce logement au dernier étage d'un immeuble donne la possibilité à ses occupants d'admirer la ligne d'horizon de la ville de Tokyo, tout en restant à l'écart du chaos qui y règne.

Die Entscheidung, die Wohnung als Penthouse zu gestalten, ermöglicht seinen Bewohnern, den Ausblick auf die Skyline der Stadt Tokio genießen zu können, fern dem Stress, der tatsächlich die Stadt auszeichnet.

Y.S HOUSE

YAMANO GUESTHOUSE AND RESIDENCE

EDWARD SUZUKI ASSOCIATES

Tokyo, Japan. 2001

The functional program for this residence demanded the reservation of a private area for guests on the first two floors of the building, while the upper floors would hold three residences for the rest of the family. The protection of personal privacy is one of the virtues of this project, whose spatial development is based on a number of large terraces used as "insulation" which organize the different areas. Just as the interior spaces are protected, so it is with the façade: a glass membrane and a row of trees act as a sieve between the house and its surroundings.

Le plan fonctionnel de ce bâtiment exigeait la présence de salles privées pour les invités au rez-de-chaussée et au premier étage, les deux étages supérieurs étant composés de trois résidences réservées au reste de la famille. Le respect de l'intimité est l'un des avantages de ce projet, dont l'aménagement spatial est basé sur de grandes terrasses à la manière d'"isolants" qui organisent les différentes ambiances. De même que les espaces intérieurs, la façade est protégée : une surface vitrée et des arbres servent d'écran entre la maison et les alentours.

Das funktionelle Programm dieses Wohnhauses forderte die Schaffung eines privaten Bereiches für Gäste auf den ersten zwei Etagen des Gebäudes, während die oberen Etagen drei Wohnungen für die Familie beherbergen sollten. Die Bewahrung der Privatsphäre ist einer der Vorzüge dieses Projektes, dessen räumliche Gestaltung auf großen Terrassen basiert, die als "Isolierung" zwischen den verschiedenen Bereichen dienen. Die Privatsphäre wird nicht nur zwischen den Innenräumen sondern auch zur äußeren Umgebung durch eine verglaste Fassade und Bäume bewahrt.

The formal treatment proposed creates a sieve between the house and its surroundings. Nonetheless, the outline of the structure can be clearly perceived at night when the house becomes transformed into an enormous, green-tinted glass lantern.

Le traitement des formes proposé ici donne naissance à un écran entre la maison et son environnement. On peut cependant percevoir nettement la volumétrie pendant la nuit, quand la maison se transforme en une grande lanterne verdoyante de verre.

Obwohl durch die formelle Gestaltung ein Filter zwischen dem Gebäude und seiner Umgebung geschaffen wird, ist die Volumetrie nachts klar erkennbar, wenn sich das Haus in eine große grüne Glaslaterne verwandelt.

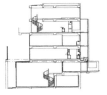

Protecting the privacy of a dwelling is one of the fundamental themes to be resolved. Thus in this case the elements used to preserve this intimacy convert this project into an attractive play of light and shadow.

L'intimité dans une maison est l'un des points les plus importants à résoudre. Les éléments utilisés ici pour la préserver permettent de créer à l'intérieur de ce projet un fascinant jeu d'ombres et de lumières.

Der Erhalt der Privatsphäre in einem Wohnhaus ist eines der bedeutendsten Themen, die beim Entwurf zu klären sind. In diesem Fall wurde dies durch den Einsatz bestimmter Elemente gelöst, wodurch das Projekt außerdem durch ein stilvolles Spiel zwischen Licht und Schatten besticht.

ZACHARY HOUSE

STEPHEN ATKINSON ARCHITECT

Louisiana, USA. 1995 / 1999

The structure of a dwelling intended for continuous use varies considerably from that of a dwelling which is only used occasionally or during vacations. For this residence in Zachary, the surrounding farms and thinly inhabited residential areas, its occasional use and "self-construction" were important factors which influenced in the proposal. Its architecture is based on the design scheme used in the typical houses of the region, which are arranged into two separate spaces ventilated through a hollow central core. In this case, the two spaces house the public and private areas respectively, while the hollow centre becomes a "third bedroom" which intensifies the relations between the house and its surroundings.

La typologie d'un bâtiment à usage permanent varie considérablement de celle d'une maison utilisée occasionnellement ou pour les vacances. Les fermes et les zones résidentielles de faible densité qui l'entourent, son utilisation peu fréquente et "autoconstruction" ont été des facteurs importants dans l'élaboration de ce projet, situé à Zachary. L'architecture est ici basée sur le schéma utilisé pour les maisons traditionnelles de la région, qui s'organisent en deux espaces séparés et aérés au moyen d'un vide central. Dans le cas présent, les deux espaces abritent la zone publique et privée respectivement, alors que le vide central devient une "troisième chambre", qui intensifie la relation entre la maison et le milieu environnant.

Es besteht ein eindeutiger Unterschied in der Typologie zwischen den ständig genutzten Wohnhäusern und den vorübergehend bewohnten Ferienhäusern. Die Planung dieses Wohnhauses in Zachary wurde durch entscheidende Faktoren beeinflusst, wie die Umgebung mit Farmen und Wohngebieten mit geringer Einwohnerzahl, seine gelegentliche Nutzung und der "Selbstbau". Seine Architektur basiert auf einem für die typischen Häuser der Region genutzten Schema, demzufolge die Gebäude in zwei getrennte Abschnitte aufgeteilt sind und durch einen zentralen freien Bereich belüftet werden. In diesem Fall beherbergen die zwei Abschnitte jeweils einen öffentlichen und einen privaten Bereich, während der zentrale Bereich zu einem dritten Abschnitt wird, durch den der Bezug des Hauses zum Standpunkt verstärkt wird.

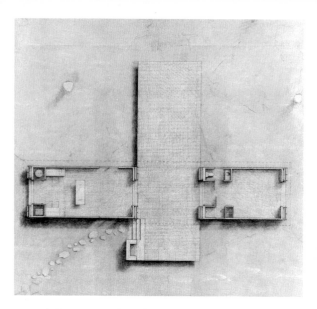

The floor plan, based on the typical local architecture, is divided into two spaces which are joined across a hollow central axis, which also serves to generate a strong visual and physical connection with the surroundings.

L'étage, basé sur l'architecture typique de la région, est réparti en deux espaces reliés à travers un axe central vide, qui crée un fort lien visuel et physique avec le site.

Nach dem Grundriss, der auf der typischen Architektur des Standortes basiert, wird das Gebäude in zwei Abschnitte geteilt, die durch einen zentralen freien Bereich verbunden werden, durch den wiederum eine starke optische und physische Verbindung zum Standort entsteht.

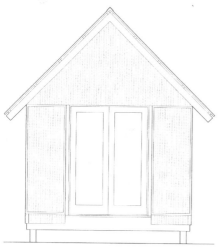

The composition of the house is formed by axes in two different directions, which are completed by the presence of a chimney. This element is the reference piece connecting the house to its surroundings.

La composition de la maison forme deux axes directionnels que la présence d'une cheminée vient compléter. Cet élément constitue la pièce de référence de la maison par rapport à l'emplacement où elle se trouve.

Das Hauses wird durch zwei gerichtete Achsen gegliedert, die durch einen Kamin vervollständigt werden. Dieses Element ist der Bezugspunkt des Hauses zum Standort.

Directory · Carnet d'adresses · Adressen

Emilio Ambasz & Associates
8 East 62nd Street
New York, NY 10021-7217
USA
① 1 212 751 3517
Fax 1 212 751 0294
www.ambasz.com

Artigues & Sanabria
Arquitectes
Aribau, 230-240 8 X
08006 Barcelona
España
① 34 93 414 4200
Fax 34 93 414 4190

Atelier Ko Architects
17 Burntwood Court,
Burntwood Lane
London SW17 0AH
United Kingdom
① 44 20 8944 5175
Fax 44 20 8944 5175
www.atko.macunlimited.net

Stephen Atkinson
c / o Studio Atkinson
526 W 11 3th St. # 74
New York, NY 10025
USA
① 1 646 698 3881
Fax 1 646 698 3811
www.studioatkinson.com

Augustin und Frank
Architekten
Schlesische Str. 29-30
10997 Berlín
Deutschland
① 49 612 843 57 / 58
Fax 49 612 843 59
augustin_und_frank@t-online.de

B & E Baumschlager-Eberle
Lindauerstrasse 31
A-6911 Lochau
Austria
① 43 55 74 4 30 79
Fax 43 55 74 4 30 79 30
office@be-g.com

BAAS Arquitectos
Frederic Rahola 63
08032 Barcelona
España
① 34 93 3580111
Fax 34 93 3580194
info@jordibadia.com

BBP Architects
93 Kerr Street
Fitzroy. VIC 3065
Australia
① 61 3 9416 1486
Fax 61 3 9416 1438
www.bbparchitects.com

Behnisch & Partner
Gorch-Fock Strabe 30
70619 Stuttgart (Sillenbuch)
Deutschland
① 49 711 47656 0
Fax 49 711 47656 56
www.behnisch.com

Mario Botta architetto
Via Ciani 16
6904 Lugano
Switzerland
① 41 91 972 8625
Fax 41 91 9701454
www.botta.ch

Döring Dahmen Joeressen
Architekten
Hansaallee 321
40549 Düsseldorf
Deutschland
① 49 211 5375530
Fax 40 211 53755375
www.ddj.de

(EEA) Erick van Egeraat
Associated Architects
Calandstraat 23
3016 CA Rotterdam
The Netherlands
① 31 10 436 9686
Fax 31 10 436 9573
www.eea-architects.com

STEVEN EHRLICH ARCHITECTS
10865 Washington Blvd.
Culver City, CA 90232
USA
① 1 310.838.9700
Fax 1 310.838.9737
www.s-ehrlich.com

ESTUDI MASSIP-BOSCH
ARQUITECTES
Ríos Rosas 47
08006 Barcelona
España
① 34 93 2112268
Fax 34 93 2112268
emb.st@coac.net

ESTUDIO CARLOS FERRATER
Bertrán 67 bajos-jardín
08023 Barcelona
España
① 34 93 4189565
Fax 34 93 2120466
ferrater@coac.es

ARCHITEKT DI ERNST GISELBRECHT
Sparkassenplatz 2 / III
80 10 Graz
Österreich
① 43 316 817050
Fax 43 316 817050-9
arch.giselbrecht@styria.com

GLUCKMAN MAYNER ARCHITECTS
250 Hudson Street
New York, NY 10013
USA
① 1 212 929 0100
Fax 1 212 929 0833
www.gluckmanmayner.com

MARK GUARD ARCHITECTS
161 Whitfield Street
London W1T 5ET
United Kingdom
① 44 20 7380 1199
Fax 44 20 7387 5441
www.markguard.com

HARIRI & HARIRI
18 East 12 Street
New York, NY 10003
USA
① 1 212 727 0338
Fax 1 212 727 0479
www.haririandhariri.com

ITSUKO HASEGAWA ATELIER
1-9-7 Yushima, Bunkyo-ku
Tokyo 113-0034
Japan
① 81 3 3818 5470
Fax 81 3 3818 1821
Iha-sec@mx1.nisiq.net

HEIKKINEN-KOMONEN ARCHITECTS
Kristianinku 11-13
00170 Helsinki
Finland
① 358 9 75102111
Fax 358 9 751 02166
www.heikkinen-komonen.fi

IZQUIERDO, LEHMANN, CIA
Isidora Goyenechea 3356, of. 41
Las Condes, Santiago
Chile
① 56 2320573
Fax 562341020
www.izquierdolehmann.co.cl

KAJIMA CORPORATION
KI Bldg
5-30, Akasaka 6-Chome
Minato-Ku, Tokyo 107-8502
Japan
① 81 3 5561 2111
www.kajima.co.jp

KISHO KUROKAWA ARCHITECT
& ASSOCIATES
11th Floor Aoyama Building
1-2-3 Kita Aoyama, Minato-ku
Tokyo 107-0061
Japan
① 81 3 3404 3481/8
Fax 81 3-3404-6222
www.kisho.co.jp

LEGORRETA + LEGORRETA
Palacio de Versalles 285-A
Mexico D.F 11020
Mexico
☎ 52 5251 9698
Fax 52 5596 6162
legorret@lmasl.com.mx

m³ ARCHITECTS
74 Great Eastern Street
London EC2A 3JG
United Kingdom
☎ 44 20 7729 4222
Fax 44 20 7729 4333
www.m3architects.com

MACK ARCHITECT(S)
2343 Eastern Court
Venice, CA 90291
USA
☎ 1 310.822.0094
Fax 1 310.822.0019
www.markmack.com

MAKI AND ASSOCIATES
13-4 Hachiyama-cho
Shibuya-ku, Tokyo
Japan 150-0035
☎ 81 3 3780 3880
Fax 81 3 3780 3881

MAP ARQUITECTOS.
JOSEP LLUÍS MATEO
Passeig de Gràcia 108 6° 1
08008 Barcelona
España
☎ 34 93 2186358
Fax 34 93 2185292
www.mateo-maparchitect.com

ELENA MATEU POMAR
Numància 73, 1.b.
08029 Barcelona
España
☎ 34 933638064
e.mateu@coac.es

MVRDV (Winy Maas,
Jacob van Rijs, Nathalie de Vries)
Postbus 63136,
3002 JC Rotterdam,
The Netherlands
☎ 31.10.4772860
Fax 31.10.4773627
www.mvrdv.archined.nl

ERIC OWEN MOSS ARCHITECTS
8557 Higuera Street
Culver City, California
90232 USA
☎ 1 310 839 1199
Fax 1 310 839 7922
www.ericowenmoss.com

MURDOCK YOUNG ARCHITECTS
526 W. 26th Street, Suite 616
New York, NY 10001
USA
☎ 1 212 924 9775
Fax 1 212 924 9865
www.murdockyoung.com

RUDY RICCIOTTI
3 pl estienne d'orves
83150 Bandol
France
☎ 33 4 94 29 52 61
Fax 33 4 94 32 45 25

SANAA LTD. / KAZUYO SEJIMA,
RYUE NISHIZAWA & ASSOCIATES
7-A, 2-2-35 Higashi-Shinagawa
Shinagawa-ku, Tokyo
140-0002 Japan
☎ 81 3 3450 1754
Fax 81 3 3450 1757
press@sanaa.co.jp

ÁNGEL SÁNCHEZ-CANTALEJO
VICENTE TOMÁS
Via Roma N° 5 1° 1ª
07012 Palma de Mallorca
España
☎ 34 617 70 00 00
sct@sctarquitectos.com

SETH STEIN ARCHITECTS
15 Grand Union Centre
West Row Ladbroke Grove
London W10 5AS
United Kingdom
☎ 44 20 8968 8581
Fax 44 20 8968 8591
www.sethstein.com

SIDNAM PETRONE GARTNER
ARCHITECTS
136 West 21st Street
New York, NY 10011
USA
☎ 1 212 366 5500
Fax 1 212 366 6559
www.spgarchitects.com

ALVARO SIZA, ARQUITECTO
Rua Do Aleixo, 53. 2o
4150-043 Porto
Portugal
☎ 351 22 6167270
Fax 351 22 6167279
Siza@mail.telepac.pt

WERNER SOBEK INGENIEURE
Albstrasse 14
70597 Stuttgart
Deutschland
☎ 49 711 767500
Fax 49 711 7675044
www.wsi-stuttgart.com

SOUTO MOURA ARQUITECTOS
R. do Aleixo, 53. 1º A
4150-043 Porto
Portugal
☎ 351 22 618 7547
Fax 351 22 610 8092
souto.moura@mail.telepac.pt

CRAIG STEERE ARCHITECTS
Suite 9, 219 Onslow Road
Shenton Park
Western Australia 6008
☎ 61 8 9380 4662
Fax 61 8 9380 4663
craig@craigsteerearchitects.com.au

EDWARD SUZUKI ASSOCIATES INC.
Maison Marian 3F, 15-23,
1-chome Seta, Setagaya-ku
Tokyo 158-0095
Japan
☎ 81 3 3707 5272
Fax 81 3 3707 5274
www.edward.net

UdA (UFFICIO DI ARCHITETTURA)
Via Valprato 68
10155 Torino
Italia
☎ 39 11 2489489
Fax 39 11 2487591
www.uda.it

ARCHITECTENBUREAU
K. VAN VELSEN
Postbus 1367
1200 BJ Hilversum
The Netherlands
☎ 31 35 6222000
Fax 31 35 6288991
kvv@architecten.A2000.nl

ARCHITEKT ALEXANDER VOIGT
Schlossstrasse 15
52066 Aachen
Deutschland
☎ 49 241 534071
Fax 49 241 534473

SHOEI YOH + ARCHITECTS
1-12-30 Heiwa, Minami-ku
Fukuoka-shi 815-0071
Japan
☎ 81 92 521 4782
Fax 81 92 521 6718
yohshoei@jade.dti.net.jp

Markku **A**latalo (House Kosketus "Touch")
©Satoshi Asakawa (Another Glass House between
sea and sky)
©Artigues & Sanabria (Casa Casadevall)
©M. Armengol (Casa Casadevall)
©Alejo **B**agué (Casa A-M; Casa en Santa Margarita;
Casa Tagomago)
©Richard Barnes (Residential House in Montana;
Thomas Residence)
©Daniel K. Brown (Residential House in Montana)
©Behnisch & Partner, Christian Kandzia
(Wohnhaus Wegmann)
©BBP Architects (Mt. Martha Beach house)
©Emilio **C**onti (Levis House)
©Richard **D**avies (New Guild House; Villa Maria)
©Serge Demailly (Villa Le Goff)
©Takeo Dec. (Takahata House)
©Peter **E**der (Wohnhaus Flachs)
©Steven Ehrlich Architects (Canyon Residence)
©Robert **F**rith / Acorn Photo Agency
(Shenton Park Residence)
©DI Ernst **G**iselbrecht (Wohnhaus Flachs; Wohnhaus
Hermann; Wohnhaus Papst; Wohnhaus Taucher)
©**H**eikkinen-Komonen Architects
(House Kosketus "Touch")
©Chipper Hatter (Zachary House)
©Roland Halbe/artur (Casa Rojas; Haus R128)
©Hiroyuki Hirai (Furniture House 1)
©Eduard Hueber (Algaier-Gaugg House;
Böhler-Jutz House; Residential House Flatz; Kern House)
©Werner Huthmacher/artur (Viesel House)
©**I**zquierdo, Lehmann (Casa Mahns; Casa Tagle)
©Nicholas **K**ane (House on Borneo Sporenburg-Plot 12;
House on Borneo Sporenburg-Plot 18)
©Furutate Katsuaki (N House; Sekine Dental Clinic and
Residence; Shiga Residence; Yamano Guesthouse
and Residence)
©Toshiharu Kitajima (INB House)
Koji Kobayashi (O Residence)
©Akira Koyama (Takahata House)
©Kisho Kurokawa Architect & Associates
(O Residence; Spanish House)
©**L**ofthouse Photography (Cottesloe Residence)
©Lourdes Legorreta (Casa Cordova; Casa Howe;
Casa La Cruz; Casa Las Terrazas)

©Estudi **M**assip-Bosch Arquitectes (Casa Tí y Ció)
©m³ Architects (Holly Bush House)
©Christian Michel (Villa Le Goff)
©Daisuke Mimura (Takahata House)
©Murdock Young Architects (Cutler Residence;
Teich Residence)
©Duccio Malagamba (Casa en la Costa Mediterránea;
Santo Ovidio Estate; Vos House)
©Ryuzo Masunaga (Residential House in Montana)
©Manos Meisen (Wohnhaus Köln-Müngersdorf)
©Michael Moran (Private Residence in Harrison)
©Pino Musi (Villa a Bernareggio)
©Robertino **N**ikolic/artur (Residence Meerbusch)
©Tomio **O**hashi (YS House; Spanish House)
Chris Ott (Mt. Martha Beach house)
©Paul Ott (Wohnhaus Flachs; Wohnhaus Hermann;
Wohnhaus Papst; Wohnhaus Taucher)
©Eric Owen Moss Architects (Sagaponac House)
©Henry **P**lummer (Stainless Steel House
with Light Laticce)
©Eugeni Pons (Casa CH)
©Undine Pröhl (House in the Perifery)
©Sharon **R**isedorph (Soma House)
©Christian Ritchers (De Held Groningen)
©Philippe Ruault (Villa Lyprendi; Villa Marmonier)
©Tiggy Ruthven (New House in Galway)
©Richard **S**canlan (Residential House in Montana)
©Jason Schmidt Photographs (Greenwich House)
©Jay Seastrunk (Cutler Residence)
©Shinkenchiku-sha (INB House; N House)
©Shoei Yoh + Architects (Stainless Steel House
with Light Laticce)
©Filippo Simonetti (House in Besazio)
©Yoshio Siratori (Stainless Steel House
with Light Laticce)
©Teresa Siza (Casa Na Serra da Arrábida)
©Eduardo Souto de Moura (Casa Na Serra da Arrábida)
©Hisao Suzuki (Weekend House)
©Stefan **T**hurmann (Wohnhaus Wierich)
Jussi Tiainen (House Kosketus "Touch")
©Hiroshi **U**eda/ Shinkenchiku-sha (Another Glass House
between sea and sky)
©Héctor **V**elazco (Casa en La Punta)

This book was made possible thanks to the collaboration of the people who have been directly and indirectly related to this project and, above all, to the architectural firms who have provided us with the material. We wish to extend our gratitude to all of them for their collaboration and most especially to:

Cet ouvrage a été possible grâce à la collaboration des personnes liées directement ou non à ce projet, et surtout aux bureaux d'architecture qui ont mis leur matériel à notre disposition, que nous tenons à remercier pour leur collaboration. Nous remercions tout particulièrement :

Dieses Buch wurde dank der Mitarbeit aller der Personen möglich, die sich direkt oder indirekt an diesem Projekt beteiligt haben, vor allem aber durch die Unterstützung der Architekturbüros, die uns das notwendige Material zur Verfügung gestellt haben. Darum gilt unser besonderer Dank:

Ariel Asken (Mack architects)
Stephen Atkinson
David Balestra-Pimpini (BBP Architects)
Richard Barnes
Jonathan Bell (Mark Guard LTD Architects)
Nuria Bermudez (Estudi Massip-Bosch Arquitectes)
Renate Blauth (Behnish & Partner)
Amy Butterworth (Emilio Ambasz & Associates)
Isabel Castro (Alvaro Siza arquitecto)
Marta Cervelló (MAP arquitectos)
Beth Cook
Richard Davies
Prof. Wolfgang Döring (Döring Dahmen Joeressen Architekten)
Ing. Eisenberger (Ernst Giselbrecht Architekt)
Ute Frank (Augustin und Frank Architekten)
Carola Franke-Hoeltzerman (Behnish & Partner)
Ernst Giselbrecht Architekt
Rachel Greenfield (Seth Stein Architects)
Gabriela Grisi (Legorreta + Legorreta)
Caroline Hansberry (Sidnam Petrone Gartner Architects)
Gisue Hariri
Chipper Hatter
Frank Heinlein (Werner Sobek Ingenieure)
Machiko Hoshino (Kisho Kurokawa Architect & Associates)
Luis Izquierdo
Nadi Jahangiri (m³ architects)
Pippa James (Seth Stein Architects)
Nicholas Kane
Markku Komonen
Antti Könönen (Heikkinen-Komonen Architects)
Hiromi Kouda (Maki and Associates)

Akira Koyama (Atelier Ko)
Kisho Kurokawa
Nack Lee (Hariri & Hariri)
Antonia Lehmann
Annemarie Magré ((Koen Van Velsen Architectenbureau)
Fumihiko Maki
Enric Massip
Elena Mateu
Adriana Miranda (Souto Moura Arquitectos Lda)
Ayako Miyamoto (Itsuko Hasegawa Atelier)
Christina Monti (Steven Ehrlich Architects)
Taeko Nakatsubo (SANAA Ltd)
Jenny Nolan (Murdock Young Architects)
Rebeca Pardo
Chrystèle Parra (Rudy Ricciotti Architecte)
Paola Pellandini (Studio Architetto Mario Botta)
Eileen Quinlan
Markus Randler (Hariri & Hariri)
Fabio Ricci
Christian Ritchers
Rocio (Artigues & Sanabria)
Catrin Schal (EEA) Eric Van Egeraat associated architects)
Hannah K.Slama (Eric Owen Moss Architects)
Hanneke Slee (MVRDV)
Craig Steere
Edward Suzuki (Edward Suzuki Asociates)
Mona Tellier
Mercedes Trias de Bes (Estudio Carlos Ferrater)
Alexander Voigt
Judith Wirthensohn (B & E Baumschlager-Eberle)
Mori Yasuyoshi (Kajima Corporation)
Koji Yokoi (Shoei Yoh + Architects)